Living When a Young Friend Commits Suicide

Selected Other Books by Earl A. Grollman

*Bereaved Children and Teens: A Support Guide for Parents and
    Professionals* (editor)
Caring and Coping When Your Loved One Is Seriously Ill
Concerning Death: A Practical Guide for the Living (editor)
Explaining Divorce to Children (editor)
In Sickness and in Health: How to Cope When Your Loved One Is Ill
Living When a Loved One Has Died
*Straight Talk about Death for Teenagers: How to Cope with Losing
    Someone You Love*
Suicide: Prevention, Intervention, Postvention
Talking about Death: A Dialogue between Parent and Child
*Talking about Divorce and Separation: A Dialogue between Parent
    and Child*
The Working Parent Dilemma (with Gerri L. Sweder)
Time Remembered: A Journal for Survivors
What Helped Me When My Loved One Died
When Someone You Love Has Alzheimer's: The Caregiver's Journey
    (with Kenneth S. Kosik, M.D.)
When Your Loved One Is Dying
Your Aging Parents: Reflections for Caregivers
    (with Sharon Grollman)

Living When a Young Friend Commits Suicide

Or Even Starts Talking about It

Earl A. Grollman and Max Malikow

Beacon Press, Boston

Beacon Press
25 Beacon Street
Boston, Massachusetts 02108-2892
www.beacon.org

Beacon Press books
are published under the auspices of
the Unitarian Universalist Association of Congregations.

Printed in the United States of America

05 04 03 02 01 00 99   8 7 6 5 4 3 2 1

This book is printed on recycled acid-free paper that contains at
least 20 percent postconsumer waste and meets the uncoated paper
ANSI/NISO specifications for permanence as revised in 1992.

Text design by Preston Thomas
Composition by Wilsted & Taylor Publishing Services

Library of Congress Cataloging-in-Publication Data

Grollman, Earl A.
    Living when a young friend commits suicide or even starts
talking about it / Earl A. Grollman and Max Malikow.
        p. cm.
    SUMMARY: Discusses why people commit suicide, how to
deal with the various emotions caused by the suicide of someone
you know, how to help someone suicidal, religious issues, and
popular misconceptions about suicide.
    ISBN 0-8070-2502-X
    1. Youth—Suicidal behavior—Psychological aspects Juvenile
literature.   2. Suicide—Psychological aspects Juvenile literature.
3. Teenagers and death Juvenile literature.   4. Bereavement in
adolescence Juvenile literature.   5. Grief in adolescence Juvenile
literature.   [1. Suicide.]   I. Malikow, Max.   II. Title.
HV6546 .G76   1999
362.28'3'0835—dc21   99-14820

In this life we will come across many obstacles on the long road to true happiness. There is responsibility which limits us, lies which mislead us, desire which distracts us, and love which sustains us.

Rachel Joy Malikow, age 13

Contents

Introduction

One of your friends or relatives has committed suicide. That's why you are reading this book. If we were with you, you could tell us about your friend. If we were with you, you could tell us how much this person meant to you. You could tell us what it feels like to have this person taken from you. You could tell us what you're thinking and ask us questions about suicide.

Since we're not with you, we've written this book for you. In it we answer the questions you're likely to ask after a friend has committed suicide:

- ☐ "Why did he kill himself?"
- ☐ "Could I have prevented it?"
- ☐ "Did I do anything to cause it?"
- ☐ "Was it really a suicide?"
- ☐ "Whose fault is it?"
- ☐ "What am I supposed to feel?"
- ☐ "Sometimes I feel depressed."
- ☐ "Could I commit suicide?"
- ☐ "Was she crazy?"
- ☐ "What happens to people when they die?"
- ☐ "Is suicide a sin?"
- ☐ "Is it wrong for me to feel angry?"
- ☐ "Why do I feel guilty?"
- ☐ "Why do people have to suffer so much that they kill themselves?"
- ☐ "How can I prevent another suicide?"
- ☐ "Is it o.k. to talk about his suicide?"
- ☐ "Do a lot of people kill themselves?"
- ☐ "Why do people kill themselves?"

Although we've tried to be thorough perhaps we've not answered all of your questions or talked about all of the things that are on your mind. This is why we've included suggestions for people you can talk to and other books you can read.

As you read this book, it would be helpful for you to remember that recovering from the death of someone you care about is a process. When that death is a suicide, it takes even more time to recover. Eventually, your pain, confusion, and sadness will decrease. A suicide kills one person and wounds those who are left behind to mourn. We've written this book to help you in your healing.

In this book, when we write "friend," you may need to substitute "brother," "sister," or "cousin." What we've written to those who have lost a friend also applies to you if you've lost a young relative.

This book is intended to help you by answering questions you have about your friend's suicide. Probably, this book includes answers to questions you are not asking. That's why we've designed this book so that it is not necessary to read it completely from beginning to end. We've written it in such a way that you can go to the table of contents, find the parts of the book that interest you, and be helped by reading those parts.

Chapter One

The First Days after a Death:
What You May Feel

Maybe it was a friend who called you and began with, "You're not going to believe what happened!" Maybe the principal of your school called an assembly and announced that he had very sad news to report. Perhaps your mother came into your bedroom, sat on your bed, and said, "I have something to tell you." However it was, you will never forget how you heard that your friend committed suicide.

Grief is a feeling that includes other feelings. One person described his grief as "cold, burning pain." A famous writer, C. S. Lewis, wrote, "No one ever told me that grief felt so like fear." What are you feeling? Shock? Depression? Loneliness? Confusion? Panic? Anger? You may be having many strange, weird, and even contradictory reactions to the shocking news. You might even have gotten physically sick when you heard of your friend's suicide.

Every death is painful for those who experience the loss. But no death is more painful and problematic than a suicide. A key to coping with the loss of someone who has committed suicide is understanding why young people deliberately end their lives. Part of life is making sense of our experiences—both sad and happy. Making sense of your friend's suicide will not be accomplished easily or completely. It is important that you realize that you will never completely understand why your friend killed himself. Sometimes it will seem that each question you answer creates two new ones. Be prepared to be frustrated at times.

Also, it will help you in your grief to understand what you are feeling and why. Identifying, understanding, and experiencing your feelings will take time. Mourning is a process. In time, it's likely you will feel sadness less often and with less intensity. Eventually you will notice that you need less time to recover from your times of sadness. Expect to feel a variety of emotions. Expect questions to accompany these emotions.

Shock and disbelief

When you first heard of your friend's suicide, you may not have felt anything. Perhaps you are still in a numb state. Do you feel bad about not feeling anything? Feeling bad is a feeling! Being numb after receiving bad news or experiencing a tragedy is not unusual. If you are in a state of shock you are getting yourself ready to feel something.

Your friend has killed herself! You are alive. You have a life to live. You have things to do. Following a tragedy, if we have responsibilities that must be met, one way to meet them is to become like robots. Going about life automatically is a temporary state. Gradually you will again experience feelings, and eventually what you feel you may feel strongly. But for now you must function, and numbness enables you to do that.

When you first enter a dark room or turn off the lights, you are unable to see. Have you ever noticed that gradually you become able to see in the dark? At first your eyes are not prepared for the sudden change. Then, without your realizing it, parts of your eyes make adjustments that enable you to see in the dark. For many the mourning process begins with shock and numbness followed by adjusting to a new environment—an environment that will never again include the person who has died.

Confusion and panic

A reaction is not the same thing as a response. Like a reflex, a reaction does not involve thought. Responses involve thinking. Reactions come from the heart, where things are felt. Responses come from the head, where things are known. Here are some reactions you may have experienced when you heard of your friend's suicide:

- □ "Oh, no!"
- □ "Oh, my God!"
- □ "It can't be!"
- □ "You're kidding!"
- □ "That's not funny!"
- □ "He was fine, I talked to him yesterday!"

Responses follow reactions. After you've had time to absorb the reality of your friend's suicide and think about what you've been told, you will have some responses. Here are some responses you might have:

- □ "Who decided this was a suicide?"
- □ "Did she leave a suicide note?"
- □ "Maybe it was an accident."
- □ "Maybe it was a murder made to look like suicide."
- □ "We talked about what we were going to do this weekend. How could she have killed herself?"

You have every right to ask questions and suggest possibilities. Part of coping with the loss of someone to suicide is needing to be convinced that it was truly a suicide. Some people ask questions sooner than others. Some people ask more questions than others. There will always be a few people who ask no questions. People in mourning must be allowed to be who they are.

Are you going crazy?

Do you feel disorganized? Does your mind wander? Do you catch yourself looking for your friend in a crowd or thinking you've seen him walking down the street? Did you start to dial his phone number and then realize, "What am I doing? I'm calling a dead person on the phone!" Are you afraid that you're going crazy?

You're not! You are adjusting to a life that no longer includes your friend. Adjustments take time. Distractibility, forgetting, imagining, and even calling out a friend's name are not unusual experiences of people in mourning. You are not going crazy.

Shame

Guilt is being sorry for something you've done. Shame is being sorry for who you are. Shame is a feeling that makes you want to avoid people. It is not uncommon for the family and friends of someone who's committed suicide to feel shame.

Perhaps you feel that others have judged you as sick or strange to have a friend who killed himself. Maybe you feel that others consider you not much of a friend since it is your friend who committed suicide. You might even feel that others think you're uncaring for not being able to help your friend.

You might be reading into others some judgments you've made about yourself. Have you considered yourself sick, strange, not much of a friend, or uncaring? If you have, then you are judging yourself without mercy. One of the reasons why we've written this book is to protect you from severely punishing yourself in these ways. As you read, you will notice that in several places we remind you that it is the person who has committed suicide who is responsible for his death.

Lack of motivation

Are you having a difficult time getting back to normal? Perhaps schoolwork seems like a drag. Maybe you feel that it's important but you can't get yourself to do it. Do you no longer enjoy things that used to be fun? Are you merely "going through the motions" when playing sports, listening to music, seeing a movie, or talking with friends? Maybe you find yourself drifting off while doing these things.

A lack of motivation is a symptom of depression. Depression is an understandable reaction to the death of someone close to you. To mourn is to experience sadness. Part of this sadness is not having passion for things that used to give you pleasure. This is usually a temporary state. You will get back to enjoying things. Although your life is rather gray these days, gradually and eventually it will regain color.

Sadness

Your friend's suicide was a declaration of her sadness. To be aware of how painful life had become for her makes you sad—very sad. Longing to be with and talk to her is a painful, saddening experience.

To be mentally healthy means to have a grasp on reality. Unfortunately, some realities bring us to a place of sorrow and grief. With your friend's suicide comes the realization of the depth of his despair. It is as though his sadness has become your own. Perhaps your sadness is influencing you to ask some questions:

- □ "Sometime I wonder, 'Is it worth it all?' "
- □ "I feel so depressed. How long am I going to feel this way?"
- □ "Is this the way she felt before she killed herself?"
- □ "If there is a God, why do people suffer so much?"
- □ "None of my friends seem to be as depressed as I am. Am I abnormal?"

□ "I feel so bad for his family. I don't want to avoid them, but what am I supposed to say to them?"

Your sadness is a declaration too. It is your statement that you care. If you were to read the obituary section of the newspaper you would be indifferent to the deaths of people you didn't know. Their lives did not touch yours. You would experience no loss at their passing. Your friend's life touched your life, and his death subtracts from your life. These are the things your sadness declares.

Fear: Could you commit suicide?

Fear is the uneasy feeling that danger or pain is near. Your friend's suicide has given you something new to be afraid of. Until your friend killed himself suicide was something other people did. Your friend is now one of the fifty thousand people in the United States who committed suicide this past year. To you, that fifty thousand is no longer a mere statistic. You know the name of one of those suicides.

You now know that sometimes a friend kills herself. This is a frightening realization. Here are some questions that sometimes accompany fear:

□ "Is there anybody else I know who is contemplating suicide? Am I going to go through this again?"

□ "Could life become so painful for me that I wouldn't want to continue living?"

□ "Am I capable of committing suicide?"

□ "I've heard that one suicide in a school leads to others. Is this true?"

□ "Is it normal for me to be afraid?"

Your fear makes sense. A tragedy that you once could only

imagine is now a reality. You'll never have to wonder what it's like to lose someone to suicide. You know what it's like. You are a suicide survivor. It's not pleasant, and it is something to be afraid of. As with all of the other feelings presented in this chapter, in time the intensity and duration of what you are feeling will diminish.

Guilt

Guilt is feeling sorry for something you've done or failed to do. It is the feeling that comes with the realization that you've failed to live up to your expectations for yourself. Here are some thoughts that arise from guilt:

- ☐ "Did I do something to cause her suicide?"
- ☐ "Could I have prevented this?"
- ☐ "Maybe if I were a better friend she would be alive."
- ☐ "Why didn't I see this coming?"
- ☐ "I knew she was thinking about suicide but I promised not to tell anyone. Was I wrong to keep that promise?"
- ☐ "I was avoiding her because she was so hard to be with."
- ☐ "I'm angry with her for killing herself. What kind of person am I to be angry with someone who committed suicide?"
- ☐ "I feel guilty when I catch myself laughing or enjoying myself."

If you promised your friend not to tell anyone about his suicidal thinking, you now regret keeping that promise. As a rule, we should keep our word. In life you will sometimes face dilemmas, situations in which you have to decide between two undesirable choices. To have to choose between breaking a promise and risking a life is a dilemma. If you feel guilty about having kept your friend's suicidality a secret, here are some thoughts for you to consider:

- [ ] It was wrong for your friend to insist that you not tell anyone. A friend shouldn't put a friend in a dilemma, especially one that involves a matter of life and death.
- [ ] "Hindsight is always twenty-twenty." Reviewing a decision knowing what followed that decision often produces guilt. The fact is you didn't know then what you know now.
- [ ] All who have a conscience experience guilt. Since guilt is an unavoidable part of life, try using it to your advantage. Learn from it and resolve not to make the same mistake again. This is how wisdom is acquired.
- [ ] You do not know for certain that if you had told someone about your friend he would be alive today. Even people who get professional help and have family support commit suicide. You'll never know what would've happened if your friend had received help.

Anger

Anger is an emotion. We are not responsible for having emotions. If we didn't have emotions we'd be like Star Trek's Mr. Spock. Having feelings is part of being a normal human being. You are responsible for understanding and managing your feelings.

One of the most difficult emotions to manage is anger. What does it mean to manage anger? It means the following:

- □ *Recognize and admit that you are angry.* Do not call your anger something else. It is not a sin to be angry. You are not a bad person for being angry.
- □ *Try to understand why you are angry.* Why does it make you angry that your friend committed suicide? You may have to talk to someone to understand your anger.
- □ *Do not express your anger at the wrong person.* This will be difficult if you are angry with your friend. *Try writing a letter to your friend.* As strange as this suggestion might seem, it is a helpful way for you to understand who you are angry with and why.
- □ *This is the time for you to deal with your anger.* If you face it now it won't take you by surprise months or even years from now.
- □ *Anger is an understandable reaction to pain.* By killing herself your friend did something that hurt you. You have a reason to be angry.
- □ *Do not allow your anger to influence you to act in a way that is cruel, destructive, or immoral.* You might be angry with your friend's parents, other family members, teachers, or friends. Perhaps you believe they are responsible for this tragedy. Take care with how you express this anger. In chapter 5, "How to Cope," we discuss a common but harmful way of expressing anger: substance abuse.

When we lose someone to whom we've been attached we feel abandoned. A person who dies abandons those who love him. A person who commits suicide has chosen his death. That choice has resulted in the pain of abandonment for you and others. Anger is an understandable reaction to someone who has given us pain. Here are some thoughts that accompany anger:

- □ "Why do I feel so angry?"
- □ "Who's responsible for this suicide?"
- □ "It has to be somebody's fault!"
- □ "Why am I so impatient?"
- □ "Why am I so easily irritated?"
- □ "I feel like being alone but resent being left alone."
- □ "I feel so lonely."
- □ "Lately I've been getting into arguments."
- □ "I feel like I'm a bad person. Why?"
- □ "I feel guilty but can't figure out what I've done."

Chapter Two

Was It Really a Suicide?

After experiencing shock from the news of your friend's suicide, you may have had questions about her death. Perhaps some of these questions are still unanswered. In this chapter we will consider the following questions:

- □ "Who decided it was a suicide?"
- □ "Could it have been an accident?"
- □ "Do a lot of people commit suicide?"
- □ "Was there a suicide note?"
- □ "My friend had plans for the future. How could this be a suicide?"
- □ "But my friend had everything to live for."

Who decided it was a suicide?

In most cases it is the medical examiner who determines that a death is a suicide. Medical examiners are unique medical doctors in that their patients are dead. Not every town or county has a medical examiner. In some places there might be a coroner who is not an M.D. In those places it is the coroner, who may be working in cooperation with a medical doctor, who determines that a death is a suicide.

In some cases it is obvious that a suicide has occurred. If death resulted from a self-inflicted gunshot, hanging, carbon monoxide poisoning, or jump from a building or bridge then the conclusion is probably unavoidable that the person committed suicide. In other cases suicide is one possible explanation among others. When it cannot be determined whether or not a death is a suicide some medical examiners and coroners will enlist the help of investigators. They will interview those who knew the deceased and had recent contact with him to reconstruct his last days. This investigation is known as a *psychological autopsy*.

Could it have been an accident?

Of course, almost anything is possible and a thorough investigation considers all possibilities. Sometimes suicide is suspected but cannot be proven. For example, some drug overdoses or automobile collisions could be either suicides or accidents. It is with reluctance that a medical examiner or coroner classifies a death as a suicide. It is likely that all other explanations for death have been ruled out before suicide is declared.

How many people commit suicide?

It is estimated that in the United States each year fifty thousand people commit suicide. Another way of expressing this number is on the average six people per hour kill themselves. Since many suicides are not reported as suicides, it is likely that the figure fifty thousand is too low.

You are a suicide survivor. If each person who commits suicide leaves behind three people in mourning, then every year one hundred and fifty thousand suicide survivors are created. This results in a total of one million suicide survivors every seven years. You are not alone.

Was there a suicide note?

Although it is commonly believed that people who commit suicide leave behind a note, research shows that only one out of four suicides includes written last words. Words do not come easily to a person in despair. Often, by the time a person has reached the point of killing himself he is so exhausted from the struggle to live that there is no energy for anything other than the final act.

Also, some suicides are impulsive acts. In these cases the struggling person sees an opportunity to kill herself and acts in the moment. For example, when walking in a subway she recognizes that she could kill herself immediately if she were to jump in front of a speeding train. In such cases, of course, there would be no suicide note.

Your friend had plans for the future. How could this be a suicide?

For every suicide that is carefully planned and carried out there is another that is impulsive. People who commit suicide go back and forth about killing themselves. One poet wrote of "decisions and revisions that a minute will reverse." Part of a suicidal person's struggle is planning for the future that he doesn't want.

But your friend had everything to live for

Have you ever heard of the *missing tile syndrome*? Imagine yourself in a bathroom that has walls and a floor made of tiles. Further imagine that this bathroom has a single missing tile. If you are like most people, it is the missing tile that would attract and hold your attention.

You were observing your friend's life from the outside. You may not have noticed any missing tiles. You saw what he had to live for. Perhaps he saw the missing tile. Maybe he obsessed over what he didn't have. If he did, then perhaps it prevented him from enjoying those things he did have.

Something else for you to consider is how well you knew your friend. You may have known her very well, but there were things about her you didn't know. Everybody lives with at least one secret. Unfortunately, often that secret is the thing a person most needs to share. You see your friend as someone who had everything to live for. Her suicide shows that she believed she had something to die for. You might not ever know what that something was.

If we've left something out: Other questions

If we've not answered a question that is important to you, find someone you think might be helpful. If you don't know of such a person ask a parent, doctor, guidance counselor, teacher, or clergy person to help you locate someone. That person might be knowledgeable about suicide, but he doesn't have to be. An intelligent, kind person who has thought about life may have wisdom to be helpful.

Most cities have a suicide crisis counseling hot-line. Check the telephone book's yellow pages under *suicide*, *crisis counseling*, or *hot-lines*. Many cities have an organization such as Contact and The Samaritans. The counselor you would speak to should be able to answer your question or direct you to someone who can.

Chapter Three

The Need to Know Why

You are a suicide survivor. A suicide survivor is anyone who has lost a relative or close friend to suicide. If you are like most suicide survivors, you want to know why your friend killed himself. Since we do not know your friend and cannot talk to you about him, we are going to share with you reasons why people may commit suicide. As you read, keep in mind that your friend might have killed himself not for one single reason, but for a combination of reasons.

Why do people commit suicide?

There are many reasons why people kill themselves. It is not enough to say that people kill themselves because they are sad. Certainly, all people who commit suicide are sad. But not all people who are sad commit suicide. What makes the difference? Here are some differences:

☐ Some people believe there's nothing they can do to make their lives better.

☐ Some people believe things about themselves that are not true.

☐ Some people are unable to stop their anger from developing into rage.

☐ Some people conclude that they are alone in the world.

Let's consider each of these differences. First, some people believe there's nothing they can do to make their lives better. This kind of thinking is called *learned helplessness*. It's the result of years of a person trying and failing to solve certain problems to improve her life. Eventually she concludes, "It doesn't matter what I do, I can't get rid of this problem and I can't live with it. The only thing for me to do is get rid of myself."

Second, some people believe things about themselves that are not true. Some people think about themselves in ways that do not square with the facts. Often, such people overreact to situations and make statements that are not logical. For example, after failing an English test you might hear someone say, "I can't do anything right, I'm a total loser." Probably he's disregarding all past success and the things he does well. Nevertheless, this is what he believes about himself.

Third, some people are unable to stop their anger from developing into rage. Rage is anger that is out of control. For reasons that can be very complicated some people get too angry. When rage is directed outward, the person who is raging might harm or even kill someone. When rage is directed inward, toward the self, the person might do harm to himself or even commit suicide.

Fourth, some people conclude that they are alone in the world. While all of us experience loneliness, few of us draw the conclusion that we have been abandoned. There is a saying, "Perception is reality." This does not mean that anything a person believes to be true is, in fact, a reality. It means that anything a person believes to be true should be taken seriously because it influences her feelings and behavior. Some people commit suicide because it is their perception that they are alone.

Was your friend crazy?

Although "crazy" is a word frequently used to describe an unusual person or behavior, it is not a word used by psychologists. If crazy means being completely out of touch with reality, then most people who commit suicide are not crazy. In fact, being in touch with reality often results in deep sadness. Famous people like the writer Ernest Hemingway, the painter Vincent van Gogh, and the poet Anne Sexton all committed suicide but were not crazy. They were people of great passion who were in touch with reality. It is not true that people who commit suicide are crazy. It is closer to the truth to state that people who commit suicide are not able to cope with their sadness.

"Bad thinking" is thinking that is negative, self-destructive, illogical, and inconsistent with reality. Bad thinking contributes to most suicides. Often, when a person is engaged in bad thinking, he cannot correct himself. Since a suicidal person cannot recognize his bad thinking and distortions of reality, he needs to talk to someone. One writer has said, "Your head's a bad neighborhood: don't go there alone." A suicidal person often cuts himself off from human contact and talks only to himself. In isolation, talking only to himself, he convinces himself that he is alone, unworthy to live, and burdened with problems he cannot solve.

Why do people get so depressed?

This is not an easy question to answer. Two people can be in what outwardly seems to be the same situation with only one of them getting depressed. Why? It is because people have different personalities and ways of interpreting events and feelings. Personality is the way a person usually thinks, behaves, and acts toward other people. For example, think of how your friends respond differently to disappointment. Some of them might be optimistic, believing that if they work hard at making things better, things will get better. Others might be pessimistic, willing to try to improve things but not expecting things to get better. Still others might be fatalistic, unwilling to even try to improve things. Like the Winnie the Pooh character Eeyore, they can be heard saying, "What's the use?"

Your personality develops throughout your lifetime from your experiences and how you understand them. Often, depressed and suicidal people are not good at solving problems. One of the reasons for this is that they've experienced a lot of failure when trying to make things better.

Another reason for depression is that misfortune is not equally distributed. Some people have more misfortune than others—and some have a good deal more than others. A lot of depression is explained by circumstances. However, usually people can tolerate the worst of situations if they are not alone. Joy shared is joy increased, pain shared is pain diminished. Holocaust survivors and American POWs in Vietnam reported that not being alone in their suffering enabled them to survive.

Depression can also result from what people expect from themselves. Unreachable goals or unreasonably high standards can lead to feelings of guilt and failure which in turn lead to depression.

If you are asking why your friend became so depressed, consider her personality and circumstances. Also consider her goals and the standards she set for herself. Perhaps this may help you to understand her depression.

Another reason why people get extremely depressed has to do with physiology. Just as hair and eye color is inherited, some people inherit depression. Depression that is inherited is much more severe than the "bad hair days" all people experience. Fortunately, since inherited depression is the result of a chemical imbalance, it can be treated with medications known as antidepressants.

It's not easy being a teenager

If you ride the school bus and there are elementary students on the bus perhaps you've caught yourself thinking, "They don't know how easy they have it." The list of responsibilities you have that they don't have looks like this:

- ☐ Getting good grades for college.
- ☐ Working part-time.
- ☐ Choosing a college or deciding on a career.
- ☐ Managing school, work, a social life, and family relationships with limited time.
- ☐ Resisting or in some other way dealing with an environment that includes alcohol, drugs, and sex.
- ☐ Separating from and being less dependent upon parents.
- ☐ Dating.
- ☐ Recognizing talents and abilities you have.
- ☐ Accepting that you don't have talents and abilities you wish you had.

Is it any wonder that the life of that second grader whose homework assignment is to collect a brightly colored leaf looks pretty good to you these days?

Suicide is a permanent solution to a temporary problem

Your friend may have looked at one or more of his problems and thought that these were permanent rather than perhaps temporary. It might be a frightening realization if you recognize similarities between the problems in your life and those in his. This may be the first time somebody you know who is your age has died. "He was too young to die!" is a common response when a young person dies. One of the ways people comfort themselves on hearing of a death is to ask, "How old was she?" If she lived ninety-five years, there may be relief in the words, "She had a good, long life." Of course, if you think about it, it's impossible for a person to be too young to die. From the moment of our first breath we are eligible for death. And a long life is not necessarily a good one.

Your friend's death reminds you not only that young people may die from illness or accidents, but that they may deliberately take their lives as well. If you are bothered by similarities between your friend's problems and your own, memorize this statement: *Suicide is a permanent solution to a temporary problem.*

Copycat or cluster suicides among teenagers

Yes, there is the fear that if you talk about suicide you only incite other unhappy, depressed people to act it out. This is often called "contagion," "copycat," "imitation," "mass," or "cluster" suicide.

The Centers for Disease Control and Prevention recommend procedures for the containment of these clusters. They suggest responsible reporting before stories leak out with misinformed gossip. Technical details of the method of suicide should be avoided to minimize the possibility of imitation by individuals contemplating suicide.

Too often, the act is described as "courageous," when the greater courage may be to do the best one can, especially when the moment is so depressing and bleak. That is why this type of death should not be glorified by flying the school flag at half-mast or erecting a permanent public memorial.

Most experts agree that grief can be worked through by acknowledging frightening feelings, identifying at-risk emotions, and seeking support and structure for appropriate expression.

All teenagers are dejected at one time or another and feel that life is just too tough. But moods change. While all of us may feel sad and lonely one day, we may feel better the next and be able to appreciate the gift of living.

Low self-esteem

Think about someone you like. Do you respect him? Do you value him as a friend? Do you enjoy being with him? Do you treat him well? Since you were thinking about someone you like, the answer to all of those questions is "yes."

People with low self-esteem have an unfavorable opinion of themselves. They don't believe they deserve respect. They don't understand why anybody would want to be with them. They don't believe they are intelligent, talented, or attractive. If they accept that they are any of those things, they believe such things are of no value. Do you see your friend in this description?

Perfectionism

For some people there are only two grades for all of life's subjects: A and F. These people are perfectionists. Perfectionists are never satisfied with themselves. Even when they've performed well they imagine how they could have done better. They never seem to have enough time and often are tired as a result of their inability to relax. Perfectionism and depression tend to occur together. No matter how good these people are, they think of themselves as losers.

Sexual issues

There are many sexual issues that have an impact on self-esteem. Inappropriate sexual encounters such as rape, incest, and harassment are some sexual issues that may cause the victim to blame herself. We prefer to believe that bad things are preventable. If we blame ourselves for something bad that happened to us, then we can prevent it from happening again in the future.

Establishing an identity as a lesbian or homosexual in our not always tolerant culture is another painful episode in our sexual development. Finding answers to the question, "Who am I?" during the identity crisis that comes with adolescence can be especially painful for gay and lesbian teenagers. After one's sexual identity is known, there is the matter of learning how to relate to other people. What behaviors are acceptable and what behaviors are unacceptable? (This is known as sexual role.)

Teenagers who are gay or lesbian are likely to experience verbal abuse, even as they are feeling stress about their sexual identity and sexual role. Such abuse can drive them into isolation or limiting their relationships. Gay youth are two to six times more likely to attempt suicide, and 30 percent of teen suicides are accomplished by lesbian and gay youth. (We say more about these issues in the section of chapter 6 on "Suicide and homosexuality.")

For the person who has been sexually abused, the memory of it remains even if the abuse stopped years ago. Nightmares, flashbacks (mental "videotape replays"), and constant nervousness often torment abuse survivors. The experience of beatings, rape, or abuse create feelings of shame and worthlessness. Many victims of such trauma view suicide as a way to escape their torment. Seeing themselves as people without value, they consider suicide an act in which nothing of value is destroyed.

Drugs and alcohol

Have you ever wondered why things as harmful and dangerous as drugs and alcohol are so popular? The explanation has to do with pain. The natural reaction to pain, either physical or emotional, is to seek relief. Taken to the extreme, the desire to have a pain-free existence results in addiction to the substance that provides relief.

Nobody intentionally becomes an addict. The road to addiction starts with occasional usage. For many, the first opportunities to use and abuse drugs and alcohol come while in junior high school. By the time high school is reached the peer group pressure to drink and drug is strong. In addition to opportunities and social pressure, there is the stress from the responsibilities of being a teenager. While it's not always easy being a teenager, try to listen to your own conscience, which has your long-term interests at heart.

There's never enough time

Let us return to that elementary school student who rides the bus with you. He's the one whose homework assignment is to find a brightly colored leaf. In contrast to him you've got a research paper to write, French vocabulary to memorize, one hundred pages of a novel to read, your college application to finish by the end of next week, and you have to try to get someone to work for you this weekend so you can go skiing with your friends. So much to do, so little time.

There was a time when your life was as uncomplicated and stress-free as that of the leaf-seeking boy on the bus. But that was so long ago that you can't even remember it any more.

School stress

In addition to the academic concerns already mentioned are decisions that must be made about school. High school juniors have to be worrying about the SAT or life after high school without college. Seniors who are going to college have numerous issues to face: What do I want to study in college? Which college offers a program in my major and is affordable? It's so expensive to go away to school, should I live at home and go to a local college? Suppose I don't get into the university of my choice?

At the same time, decisions must be made about time. Often there are questions about continuing to participate in sports, drama, yearbook, or other extracurricular activities that are time-consuming but enjoyable.

Problems with friends

Most car accidents occur within five miles of home because that's where most driving takes place. You're likely to have more relational problems with your friends than with anybody else because they're the people you interact with most. Also, if you didn't value them they wouldn't be your friends. It's a serious matter when important relationships aren't working well.

Family problems

No family situation is perfect. All families have some dysfunctionality. (Author Mary Karr has defined a dysfunctional family as "any family consisting of more than one member.") But when separation, divorce, alcoholism, physical abuse, or incest occurs, then a family is seriously dysfunctional. In a seriously dysfunctional family all members are affected. Such families need help.

Chapter Four

Facing the Immediate Future

Obviously we don't know exactly when you are reading this book. If you are wrestling with the question of whether or not to attend the funeral it means that your friend's suicide occurred within the last two days. If the funeral is past, you still might want to read the section, "Should you attend the funeral?" This part of the chapter might provide ideas for keeping alive the memory of your friend as well as things you can do that might give you comfort.

The immediate future includes contact with your friend's family. It's important that you know what a visit from you might mean to them. If you choose to visit them, we'd like to help you by suggesting things for you to say, and to avoid saying.

The immediate future also includes returning to school. This will be especially difficult if you and your friend attended the same school, making it a place of reminders and shared memories. Other reminders and shared memories, like your friend's birthday and places you once went together, are part of this chapter under "How to survive special days."

Should you attend the funeral?

It is not for us to tell you to attend the funeral. That decision should be made by you. We don't believe anybody should go to a funeral if he strongly objects to being there. Funerals are not fun and nobody wants to go to them. This especially difficult funeral might be the first funeral you've been called to go to. What we can do is to tell you why we have funerals. We'd like you to consider reasons why it would be good for you and others if you go. We realize that even if we convince you that the funeral has value and might be helpful to you, you still may feel that you cannot go.

Often it is very difficult to tell the difference between what you can't do and what you won't do.

Why do we have wakes (also known as calling-hours) and funerals? Your presence at wakes and funerals makes a statement. It states that your friend matters to you. You are saying that his life touched yours and you feel his absence. You are recognizing the value of his life, and this recognition provides support for his family. Any message to his family that they are not alone in their pain helps them. Do not underestimate the comfort provided by your presence.

You might benefit from attending the funeral as well. It would encourage you to begin the adjustment from a life that included your friend as a companion to a new life in which she is no longer available to you. With every ending comes a beginning. The wake, shiva, funeral, cemetery graveside service, and post-funeral gathering may help you conclude a relationship based on physical contact and begin one based on memory.

It might help you in making your decision if you consider the following list of reasons why we have funerals.

- ☐ They provide an opportunity to receive and express love.
- ☐ They show respect for your friend, his family, and his other friends.
- ☐ They provide you with an opportunity to share your grief among people who will understand.
- ☐ They confirm the reality that death is a part of life and the death of someone you love has occurred.
- ☐ They provide you with an opportunity to receive and give emotional support.
- ☐ They provide you with an opportunity to reflect on your friend's life and share memories with others who appreciate them.

- [ ] They provide you with evidence that you are not alone in your grief.
- [ ] They provide you with an opportunity to say good-bye to your friend on the day set aside for saying it.

Should you visit the family?

We've already said that your visit to the family would be of benefit to them. There remains the question of whether or not a visit would be good for you. One condition that would make it unwise for you to visit would be if you blame any member of your friend's family for his suicide. More than anybody else, members of the family are asking the question, "Am I to blame for his death?" Also, some family members may be blaming other family members for his suicide. If you hold any member of the family responsible for your friend's death, then we advise against a visit.

If you decide not to visit for this reason you may want to contact family members individually, either personally or in writing. (These would be those family members you don't hold responsible.) When communicating with them, it would not be helpful to share your belief about who's to blame. The question of responsibility will be addressed by the family eventually and over a long period of time.

Reasons why it might be good for you to visit the family are the same as for attending the funeral. We suggest that you reread the list of reasons why we have funerals and consider them reasons for visiting your friend's family as well. (The last reason listed would be the only exception.)

If you do visit the family, what should you say? What should you not say?

Before visiting the family, prepare yourself by answering this question: "Why do I want to make this visit?" You are ready to visit if your answer is, "To be with people who love and miss my friend so that I might give and receive comfort."

You might prepare the family for your visit by contacting them beforehand. Don't be surprised if they refuse your visit. There is no rule for how long after the funeral you should wait before making a visit. We recommend that you contact them when you feel ready. If they refuse then wait two to four weeks and call again. In that time a card or note from you saying you hope to visit later might reassure them that their child is special to you. It's likely that eventually they will want a visit from someone to whom their daughter was so special.

When you visit, you should do so confidently. We say this because you are doing the right thing. First, your desire to be with them and your presence will say more than any words you'll speak. Second, although life is going on for you, you will be taking time out to be with people who miss your friend too. You will have this in common with them.

When visiting, ask permission to share some memories of your friend. Although it is likely the family members will appreciate this, it might be too painful for them. When you speak of missing him, be specific. For example, "I miss having lunch and talking with him."

It would be better that your visit be too brief rather than too long. Conversations that are emotionally draining make people tired. There are two kinds of time: clock time and emotional time. Clock time is always the same. Emotional time varies depending upon the activity. "Time flies when you're having fun," but an hour can seem like two or three if the conversation is serious and painful. We suggest that your first visit be between a half-hour and an hour.

Don't try to make them feel better by referring to other deaths, especially suicides. It will not help them to know that others are going through the same thing. Don't say, "Well, at least she's with God and no longer suffering." They might be struggling with their religious faith, wondering where she is and why God didn't help her in a time of agony and turmoil. Don't make believe that nothing's happened. This would be denial. Remember, you'll be visiting with people who share your grief. Don't be too philosophical about the meaning of life in a world that can be cruel and where people suffer to the point of despair. Not that these aren't important questions. But because they are complex and unanswerable they do little to relieve pain. Don't say, "Is there anything I can do for you?" Your visit implies your willingness to be of help. At a time of penetrating emotional pain, people may not know what they want from others.

Returning to school after a suicide and how school can help in the mourning process

Now that your friend has committed suicide, you may dread returning to school. How can you concentrate and study as if nothing had happened? What will be the reactions of your teachers and classmates? Suppose you cry?

Just as you need to grieve *your* personal sorrow, so the school community requires an opportunity to mourn *their* tragedy. No one can ignore what happened, can they? You all need to cope in the most structured, controlled manner possible. By together acknowledging the loss you can better provide a safe place to adjust to that empty desk and locker. The first day after the suicide is usually the most chaotic, with the highest level of visible mourning.

It is advisable that you all receive from the school administration a formal statement or written memo so that accurate information is distributed before unfounded rumors begin to erupt. Know that there will be a wide range of emotions. There is no "right way to feel." Each of you will have your own unique responses. Classroom activities may need to be altered especially for the first few days after the untimely death. Talking about feelings is an appropriate way of working through grief. You might wish to go to a designated area to meet with a counselor; if you just don't feel like you can go to class, someone might be assigned to walk with you through the halls. Or you might just want to be alone in the library. Do what is best for *you*.

Most experts believe that an auditorium presentation is ineffective because of crowd control and frenetic contagion. Smaller groups are usually more manageable and organizable. You might request one-on-one counseling with the school psychologist if you feel the need.

A crisis management team can be an integral part of the grief process. (If you don't have one, now is the time to consider this crucial need.) The task force might include educators, therapists, parents, local law enforcement officers, community leaders, and students. Each will be specially trained for the trauma of suicide and better able to work out the protocols for this possibility by identifying needs and coping skills. *Planning does not encourage suicide; it allows the school to react in the most meaningful way possible in serving the needs of students and staff.*

If the funeral is being conducted during school hours, a parental note may be required for an excused absence. Whether you attend or not, you may wish to write a personal letter of condolence to the family describing some of the happier memories with your friend.

How to survive special days

It's important that you anticipate special days. Special days are any days that are likely to bring your friend to remembrance. Certainly his birthday would be a special day. If he was involved in school plays, then the opening night of the next play will be a special day. If you loved watching football games together, then his absence at the next Super Bowl party will be a special day. The day he was supposed to graduate from high school will be a special day. Any day in which his absence is obvious to you will be a special day.

Surviving special days will require that you anticipate them. If you see them coming, you won't experience a vague sense that something is wrong without knowing what it is. On special days do something special! By this we mean that you might go to the cemetery or arrange to have lunch with a member of your friend's family. You might want to arrange to have a memorial message placed in the obituary section of the newspaper. (Someone at the newspaper is available to help you with this.) Making a donation to a charity that interested her is always appreciated. A special day is a day to talk about her and what her absence means to you.

Chapter Five

How to Cope

The word "cope" is a verb, an action word, defined as "to struggle against difficulties and act to overcome them." In this chapter we suggest things for you to think about and do to overcome the difficulty of dealing with your friend's suicide.

Stress

Stress is what we feel when facing something we don't think we can manage. It is not possible to live a stress-free life. (Even that second grader on your school bus was "stressed out" about not being able to find the right leaf.) In chapter 3 we listed the things that cause stress for teenagers under "It's not easy being a teenager." You were experiencing stress before your friend killed himself.

The first thing for you to know about coping with your friend's suicide is that it's normal to feel overwhelmed and to think, "I can't handle this!" Although stress can't be measured, there's a big difference between everyday stress and the stress from your friend's suicide. The second thing we'd like you to know is that there are ways to reduce stress. Although stress can't be eliminated, it can be reduced and managed. Think of stress as a beast that can't be slain but can be tamed.

Accepting that mourning will take time

One of the world's all-time best-selling books begins with these three words: "Life is difficult." In the first page the author explains that one of the things that makes life difficult is that there are many things that cannot be hurried. Mourning is one of those things.

Mourning is the process of accepting the reality of a death, experiencing the pain that goes with it, getting used to being without someone we love, and rebuilding a new life. It takes time to accomplish all of that. It's important for you to know that. We don't want you to become impatient with yourself. Mourning takes as long as it takes. As weeks become months, you'll notice that the intensity of your pain and the duration of your sad times will decrease. That is what healing is. Don't feel guilty about healing, it's o.k. to heal.

There is good news and bad news in all of this. The bad news is that mourning will take time. The good news is that once bad news is understood and accepted it becomes less bad. Consider this question: "What kind of person would you be if you didn't feel bad for a long time following the sudden death of a friend?"

Recognizing your loss as permanent

Earlier we said that suicide is a permanent solution to a temporary problem. Your friend's permanent solution created a permanent problem for you: You will never again be with him. You will never again talk to him. A song from the animated movie *An American Tail* instructs us to "never say never." In spite of the contradiction in that statement, "never" is a word to be used rarely. However, following a friend's death, "never" is the word that describes when you will see him again. "Wish you were here!" is the thought often expressed on post cards sent by vacationers to family and friends. You can't say that to your friend; you can't even send him a post card.

How does recognizing your loss as permanent help you to cope? Part of coping is reconnecting with the present. This means resuming the activities that are a part of your life. To make the most of the present you must live in it. Life is temporary, death is permanent. Experiencing the death of someone close to us reminds us that we too will one day die. This reminder motivates us to make the most of the time we have.

Making the most of the time you have might include doing something to memorialize your friend. In the sections of chapter 4 on "Returning to school after a suicide and how school can help in the mourning process" and "How to survive special days," we suggested some ways for you to keep alive the memory of your friend.

Also, your friend left behind other suicide survivors. They too share your love for her. Reconnecting with the present and talking to others who miss her helps you to remember her and keep alive her memory.

Experiencing the pain

A famous man once amazed a crowd by holding his hand slightly above the flame of a candle. When asked how we was able to endure the pain he answered, "The trick is not to care." The pain you are feeling is because you care about your friend. It's not only pain from losing him, but also the awareness of *his* pain. His was a pain so great that he killed himself to get away from it.

It's not unusual for people in mourning to bury their pain by becoming very busy. "If I can keep myself busy," they reason, "then I won't think about her." Some people do this without realizing that's what they're doing. However, anything that's "buried alive" will scratch and claw to get to the surface. Eventually, the pain of loss will be faced.

As we mentioned, others will abuse alcohol or drugs to avoid pain. This is the road to addiction. When a person abuses alcohol or drugs to avoid pain he builds up a tolerance for them. This means that over time he will need increasing amounts of them to accomplish his goal. Eventually, what began as one problem (pain) becomes a second problem (addiction).

We aren't saying that pain is pleasant. Neither are we saying that you should seek it out and experience as much of it as you can. We are saying that experiencing pain shows that you care about someone who suffered greatly. Also, we are saying that the best way to deal with pain is to accept it as a necessary, temporary part of the mourning process. Finally, through the years many people who have suffered pain have reported that it's made them more compassionate and sensitive.

Adjusting to a world that no longer includes your friend

To miss someone is to feel his absence. When someone has died we don't miss him every moment of every day. We miss him at certain times. If it was your habit to have lunch with him then you'll miss him at lunch. If you had English class together then you're likely to notice his absence there. Your friend will come to mind when you hear his favorite song or laugh at something he'd enjoy. When you see someone on the street or in a store who resembles your friend you might even catch yourself calling out his name.

The more a person is involved in your daily life, the more often you will miss her. To lose a friend is to have one less person with whom to share good news. It means having one less person to talk to when things aren't going well. It means having one less person with whom to go places and do things. Adjusting to a world that no longer includes your friend means getting used to her absence.

We don't have any suggestions for speeding up this adjustment. As with the mourning process in general, this adjustment will be made in time as you become accustomed to daily life without your friend. You'll never entirely forget him and you wouldn't want to. An indication that he's entering your thoughts less often would be when you realize that you no longer look for him at lunch or have him come to mind when you hear his favorite song. Do you carry something of his or wear an article of his clothing to feel linked to him? When you notice that you no longer have that item with you, it may be an indicator that you're making this adjustment. However, we repeat that you'll never entirely forget your friend.

Avoiding unhealthy shortcuts: Drugs, alcohol, and isolation

Since we've already addressed the abuse of drugs and alcohol as an unhealthy way to avoid pain, we'll merely add here that alcohol is a depressant. This means that it depresses the nervous system. Although alcohol provides some temporary pain relief, when used excessively it makes a person more depressed. People who drink because they are sad make themselves sadder by drinking. The belief that alcohol reduces depression is mistaken since it actually increases both depression and drinking.

Just as drinking is part of a vicious cycle, so too with isolating. You might be closing yourself off from others because it's impossible for you to make "small talk." Your friend is dead and you miss her. You might wonder, "How can I relate to people who act as though nothing's happened?" Acting as though nothing's happened is one way some people deal with death. If you're not one of them, it's understandable that you don't want to be around them. What we caution you about is not being around anybody.

If you isolate, then you're likely to conclude that you're the only one who feels the loss of your friend. As you spend more time alone, you'll become more convinced that this is so. The fact is you're not alone. There are others who feel what you're feeling. Don't cut yourself off from them. Instead, listen for them. You'll hear them because they're around you.

Don't talk only to yourself, recycling your own thoughts. Does this concept sound familiar? It's one of the things we said about suicidal people earlier in this book. Like drinking, isolation adds to the feeling it's intended to reduce. If you've removed yourself from others in order to alleviate your pain, you're actually adding to it. You're convincing yourself that you're alone, making yourself even more depressed.

The stories of people who survived the Holocaust, Vietnam POW camps, and other situations of unimaginable suffering include the importance of human contact. These survivors all say the knowledge that they were not alone contributed to their survival.

Crying

You might be surprised to learn that there is a physiological reason why crying makes a person feel better. (Isn't it remarkable that medical researchers have studied tears?) We're not going to get into the biology and body chemistry of crying. It's more important that you remember these two words: crying helps!

What does it mean for you to cry? It means that a part of you has been touched, a part that is alive and feels. Normally functioning people have feelings, and sometimes their feelings make them cry. Singer-songwriter Paul Simon's song "I Am a Rock" includes the following words, describing someone who is determined not to be hurt again because of a relationship:

> *And a rock feels no pain.*
> *And an island never cries.*

But you are neither a rock nor an island. You are a thinking, feeling human being. While pain is not a pleasant feeling, it's part of what it means to be alive and normal. If you can't feel pain, then you won't feel anything else, including pleasure. One of the ways we express pain is by crying. People never speak of struggling to cry. Instead, they often speak of fighting to hold back tears. It's natural to cry and unnatural not to.

Perhaps you're familiar with the science fiction movie *The Terminator*. Played by Arnold Schwarzenegger, the Terminator is a robot programmed to methodically kill human beings designated for termination. In the first of the two *Terminator* movies the Terminator is described as follows: "It can't be bargained with, it can't be reasoned with. It doesn't feel pain or pity or remorse." You are neither a rock nor an island nor a science fiction cyborg. You are a person who needs to feel and perhaps cry in order to feel better eventually.

Talking

Fortunately it isn't necessary for us to understand why something is helpful in order for it to be helpful. We don't fully understand why talking is helpful. But it is. In this section we suggest three ways of talking about your friend's suicide: journaling, support groups, and professional help.

Journaling is a way of talking to yourself. You're not crazy if you talk to yourself. Everybody does it. It's merely thinking out loud. Journaling is writing down what you're thinking. Keeping a diary is a form of journaling, but you don't have to write something every day for journaling to be helpful.

Writing is helpful because the work of expressing your feelings and thoughts on paper results in a better understanding of yourself. One author has written, "I write because it helps me to make sense of it all." As we said earlier, all people try to make sense of their experiences.

Another benefit of journaling is that it gives you something to return to days, weeks, months, or even years later. On those days when you especially miss your friend you might feel that you're making no progress in your mourning. Reading from your journal might help you to see that although you feel bad today your pain has been much greater in the past.

Also, writing provides a way to release your feelings. Confusion, guilt, anger, fear, sadness, and loneliness are feelings that are normal for suicide survivors. Journaling will help you to make sense of them and feel them with less intensity.

A support group is several people and a counseling professional meeting regularly to discuss something they have in common. There are support groups for suicide survivors. For a support group to be helpful it is important that you find one that consists of people your own age who have had similar relationships to a friend who committed suicide. There are suicide survivor support groups for parents, and others for brothers and sisters. Probably it will be more difficult to find a support group for friends of a person who's committed suicide. We suggest you ask your school guidance counselor about a support group. If special counselors came to your school after your friend's suicide, then ask one of them about a group. If you can't find a group, you might want to ask one of the counselors about starting one. Don't be intimidated by the thought of starting a group. Your counselor should be able to help you.

Another way of talking about your friend's suicide is meeting with a professional. There are many types of professionals who do counseling: therapists, school guidance counselors, medical doctors, priests, ministers, and rabbis. It's not unusual for a professional who does counseling to recommend a specialist. Some counselors specialize in bereavement counseling—helping people go through the mourning process. Don't be disappointed if the person you go to refers you to another counselor who specializes in bereavement. Talking to such a person will give you more help more quickly. As we've said, mourning takes time. But you don't want it to take any more time than is necessary.

Whether you journal, attend a support group, or meet with a counselor, you will be helped by expressing your feelings and thoughts. Remember, whatever you're feeling or thinking is normal. If your feelings and thoughts seem abnormal or even crazy to you it's because of the extraordinary thing that's happened. Your friend killed herself! Although there are many suicides every year, most people are not suicide survivors. You are part of a minority, but you are not alone. One suicide is too many, but it doesn't happen often enough for anybody to get used to it. An extraordinary thing has happened and your feelings and thoughts, although normal, are unfamiliar to you. It will comfort you to share them.

Laughing

We've told you not to hold in your feelings. Just as we've encouraged you to accept and express anger, guilt, fear, and sadness, we also encourage you to laugh. To react to something that's funny is not a betrayal of your friend. Laughter provides occasional relief from your sadness. Mourning is work. It is hard, emotional work. Like every other kind of work you do, you need to take a break from it. During the Civil War Abraham Lincoln often began important meetings with a humorous story. When asked why he did this he said, "If I don't, I think my heart will break."

Your memories of your friend include times you laughed with him. You are not denying the pain of losing him when you remember the good times. Sadness is waiting for you on the other side of the laughter. Pain should not be your constant companion.

American prisoners of war in Vietnam and Jewish Holocaust survivors have reported that the ability to appreciate humor and to laugh helped them to survive. Mark Twain experienced the sorrow of his daughter's death. Yet it was Twain who said, "The true source of humor is not joy but sorrow."

Doing the next thing because it's there

We remind you that this part of the book is about how to cope, which is defined as "to struggle against difficulties and act to overcome them." Coping requires doing. "Doing what?" you may ask. "Doing something" is our answer. Often we overlook the obvious. We know of a woman whose husband was murdered. Upon receiving the tragic news she described herself as first going numb and then changing her infant daughter's diaper, "because it was the next thing to do and it needed to be done."

This woman didn't clean her house, bake a pie, or do some gardening. She did something that needed to be done immediately. Following a tragedy people live in moment-by-moment segments, doing a series of "next things." After a plane crash, the shocked survivors look for other survivors and tend to the wounded. Later they formulate a plan for getting help if they conclude that rescuers are not on the way.

In your sadness and confusion the thought of going through the remaining months of school may seem overwhelming. Don't think about the rest of the school year and the final exams that are months away. Instead, reduce your planning to the next two or three days. If you still feel overwhelmed and without direction then focus on today or just the next couple of hours. Ask your parents or some other adult you respect to help you identify the things that need to be done immediately. If you and your friend attended the same school, your teachers are prepared to postpone tests and extend deadlines. If the teachers in your school don't know about her suicide, ask your guidance counselor to speak to them about postponements and extensions. At a time like this most people will want to help you. Telling them what you need will help them to help you.

Helping others

Taking opportunities to help other people will help you to cope. When we help others we are getting outside of and going beyond ourselves. This is what we need to do when we are in pain. In fact, the pain we experience makes us more sensitive to the pain of those around us. In various ways many great thinkers have said that without the experience of pain a person cannot be compassionate.

Here again we encounter something that we cannot fully explain that will be helpful to you. We don't know why it is that helping others will have the effect of reducing your grief. Perhaps it's because helping others reduces our self-awareness at a time when the only awareness we have is of our sadness. Whatever the explanation might be, human beings are made in such a way that their sorrow is reduced when they are helping others.

You might consider getting involved in some of the following helping activities:

- □ Participating in a support group.
- □ Volunteering for a suicide crisis hot-line. (You will receive training for this.)
- □ Providing child care for a single parent.
- □ Being a friend to a lonely classmate.

☐ Visiting residents in a nursing home.

☐ Tutoring a struggling student.

You could become a wounded healer reaching out to others in their time of need.

Exercising

Although exercise is not for everybody, we encourage you to consider it. Perhaps you used to exercise but have gotten away from it. Resuming working out could be helpful for a number of reasons. First, it would be a return to a more normal life, the life you had before your friend killed himself. Second, you would be regaining control of a part of your life. Your friend's suicide was an important part of your life that you couldn't control. Third, you would be filling a part of your day with a healthy activity that could give you a break from thinking about his suicide and what it means to you.

Also, there are biological reasons why exercising is helpful. Physical exertion stimulates the body to produce a type of hormone called endorphins. (Morphine is a pain killer and the term endorphin literally means "morphine produced within the body.") Endorphins have a strong mood-elevating effect; they are responsible for the "runner's high" experienced by long-distance runners. In addition, exercise stimulates the production of adrenalin, another substance that has a mood-elevating effect.

Mourning is a time of psychological uneasiness or tension. Unless it is released, tension can cause physical problems. (Perhaps you've heard of "tension headaches.") Exercise is a way to discharge tension. If you try it, you'll notice that after working out you'll be in a more relaxed state.

Whether you exercise alone, with a partner, or as part of a larger group, make sure you choose an activity you enjoy. If you don't enjoy what you've chosen, then you're likely to skip work-outs and feel guilty about missing them. Recovering from a friend's suicide will not be the result of any one thing you do. Recovery will come in time from a combination of things. Exercise is something that has worked for others and might work for you.

A final thought is that exercise is actually controlled injury. When working out, an athlete intentionally injures muscle tissue just enough for it to recover in time for the next workout. Recovering muscle tissue knits back together a little bit stronger than it was before. This is what is happening to you psychologically in the mourning process. After recovering from your friend's suicide you'll be a stronger person.

Remembering and honoring

"Remembering and honoring those who have gone before us" is as much a part of what it means to be a human being as anything else we do. This quotation was written four days after the first Veterans Day, this country's official day for remembering the men and women who have served in the military. On the last Monday of May we celebrate Memorial Day, our national day for remembering all those who have died. In the practice of religion, Jewish people celebrate Passover to remember their liberation from slavery in Egypt, and Christians partake of the Lord's Supper (or communion) hearing the words of Jesus: "Do this in *remembrance* of me."

It isn't necessary to have a national holiday or religious celebration to remember and honor someone whose life has touched us. Recently a college student told us he planted a tree on the day his best friend died. That tree, he explained, reminds him that death is a part of life and that life goes on even when we lose someone. However, he added, it's important to remember a lost friend.

Your friend committed suicide, but there is more to her life than how it ended. Her life included actions, accomplishments, special moments, tender words, and times of laughter. Of course there was great sadness in her life; that was declared by her suicide. However, the end is not the entire story of her life. Consider remembering and honoring all of your friend's life by doing the following on her birthday or the anniversary of her death:

☐ Visiting the cemetery
☐ Reading her favorite poem or listening to her favorite song.
☐ Watching her favorite movie or a movie the two of you enjoyed together.
☐ Planting a tree.
☐ Visiting his family or getting together with his other friends.
☐ Wearing a keepsake, an article of clothing or piece of jewelry, for the day.

Remembering and honoring is very helpful in coping. Have you ever noticed that athletes wear black armbands to remember a teammate? One of the most emotional moments of the movie *Saving Private Ryan* occurs at a cemetery where an old man remembers and honors the courageous and decent man who saved his life. However you choose to do it, you will appreciate the good effect of remembering and honoring your friend.

Chapter Six

How Can You Help Suicidal People?

Whether you've experienced a friend's suicide or are close to someone who is contemplating suicide, you might be wondering whether it can be prevented. You might be asking some of the following questions:

- "How can I tell if someone is suicidal?"
- "What if I know someone who's suicidal but I've promised not to tell anyone?"
- "What if I don't know what to say to a suicidal person?"
- "Can a suicidal person be helped?"
- "Is it true that homosexuals are suicidal?"

In this chapter we respond to these questions. An important part of your recovery from your friend's suicide is learning from this tragedy. Learning how to recognize a suicidal person and knowing how to help will enable you to face the future with greater confidence and optimism. If you learn something from her suicide that prevents another one, then it will honor her life by adding meaning to it.

How you can tell if someone is suicidal

"I attempted suicide. . . . I ran the car off the cliff, and it was like a 40 . . . 30-foot drop. The car went down and hit and there wasn't a scratch on me or on the car." These are the words of professional football star Deion Sanders of the Dallas Cowboys. Sanders shocked the sports world in the fall of 1998 with his description of his attempted suicide. Who would have thought that a wealthy, famous athlete would try to kill himself? Yet, even with this unlikely candidate for suicide one of the signs was there. He had become despondent over the recent death of his father.

If you know what to look for, you can better recognize a suicidal person. A suicidal person can be identified from circumstances and clues. The circumstances are situations or conditions of his life. Clues are behaviors that suggest he is preparing to kill himself. Before continuing to read keep in mind that not everybody who is described by these circumstances and clues is suicidal. For example, not everybody whose father dies will attempt suicide as Deion Sanders did. What we present are things frequently observed in suicidal people.

Circumstances

The death of a loved one can move a person to contemplate suicide. The end of a relationship by death, especially if it was sudden, can drive a person into such despair that she sees her own death as the only way to have pain relief. She might even believe that in death she will be reunited with the one she misses.

A relationship may end not by death but by breaking up. Those who have had a boyfriend or girlfriend break up with them are not comforted by being told that the relationship wasn't that important and that they'll find somebody else. Adults need to understand that "puppy love" is a demeaning term for powerful emotions. Heartbroken people are not comforted by having someone trivialize their pain.

One of the most important conditions to consider when estimating the probability of a person's suicide is family history. If a person's family includes a suicide, especially by one of his parents, then suicide may have been planted in his mind as a way to solve problems. Suicide can become a self-fulfilling prophecy. (A self-fulfilling prophecy is when expecting something to happen makes it happen.) You must take it seriously when you hear someone say,

"I know that someday I'm going to kill myself, just like my father (or mother or brother or sister) did."

While this book was being written the following story appeared in the October 23, 1998, *Post Standard* (Syracuse, New York):

> Brett Wallace took along a .410-gauge shotgun when he drove his Suzuki Samurai to high school Wednesday morning. He found his girlfriend inside Sherburne-Earlville High School and kissed her goodbye, said Cheryl Wallace, Brett's mother.
>
> Brett Wallace ran out of school, got in his car and drove about a quarter of a mile from the school driveway. He pulled over on Collins Hill Road, took his shirt off and put the shotgun to his head.

Two days earlier, Brett Wallace had pled guilty to fourth-degree grand larceny and been sentenced to one to three years in prison. Facing imprisonment, having trouble in his relationship with his girlfriend, and no longer playing the sport he loved, football, Wallace's life was characterized by the turmoil that often precedes a suicide. In his case several conditions combined to create chaos and confusion.

Having control of our lives, which means having control of ourselves and the situations affecting us, is necessary to contentment. Anticipating a person's suicide requires an awareness of what is going on in her life. Pay attention to the friend whose circumstances may have driven her to the conclusion that the only way to regain control of her life would be to end it.

Another feature of the Brett Wallace story is the experience of humiliation. Imprisonment means not only loss of freedom and control over one's life but also shame. Humiliation can result from criminal activity, public disclosure of a private matter, failing grades, or poor performance. Guilt for having embarrassed and disappointed family and friends can accompany humiliation.

It's no small task for a person to restore his reputation and repair the damage done by misbehavior, public disclosure, or poor performance. In fact, the task of restoring and repairing might seem impossible to accomplish. It's at times like this that it will be especially difficult to convince a friend that suicide is a permanent solution to a perhaps temporary problem. At such times encourage your friend to follow the "Three Ss " of restoration:

1. Seek appropriate help. This is not the time for him to isolate or "heroically" go it alone.
2. Separate the things she can do from the things she cannot do. This is not the time to think about things over which she has no control.
3. Sequence the things to be done and direct thought, time, and energy to the next thing. This is not the time to look at everything that must be done and be overwhelmed.

Another condition that contributes to suicide is ongoing substance abuse. Heavy and increasing use of drugs and alcohol can make it easier for a person to develop a plan for suicide and act on it. Your friend doesn't have to be an addict to be influenced by substances that can cloud his judgment and enable him to act recklessly. Not all suicides are well-planned. Some suicides are impulsive acts carried out in a drunken or drugged state.

Clues

In addition to circumstances suicidal people often provide clues that they are moving in the direction of self-destruction. Indications that someone is in a process that will end in his suicide include the following:

- [ ] He's asking questions about what happens to a person who dies. Or he's showing an unusually strong interest in afterlife subjects like heaven, hell, or reincarnation.
- [ ] She's talking fatalistically, declaring the meaninglessness of life and the futility of trying to enjoy life in a world so cruel and unjust.
- [ ] He's showing a preoccupation or obsession with books, movies, poems, or songs that feature death.
- [ ] She's talking about meeting with a doctor or clergyperson without being clear about why. (Such meetings can be helpful, especially if the doctor or clergyperson knows of your friend's depression and suicidal thinking.)
- [ ] He's looking up and contacting people he's not seen for some time. (This could be to say goodbye, either directly or indirectly.)
- [ ] She's giving things away, as if to distribute remembrances to special people.
- [ ] He's isolating and showing indifference to friends and activities he used to enjoy.
- [ ] She's no longer studying and is unaffected by her dropping grades.
- [ ] He's behaving recklessly, showing no regard for the danger in high speed driving, drug overdosing, or being in the company of risk-taking people.
- [ ] She's securing the means to kill herself. (Suicidal people often acquire prescription medication and renew the prescription without using up the first prescription. This is called *stockpiling*.)
- [ ] He's choosing or insisting on staying home when his family is going away for the weekend or on vacation.

☐ She's appearing to feel better after talking about suicide or having been extremely depressed. When a person has been struggling with whether or not to continue living, the decision to commit suicide can bring relief or even happiness. This is because the decision has been made and the pain will be over soon. This is a strong clue and it is very important to remember it.

What if you've promised not to tell anyone?

If a friend approaches you saying, "I have something to tell you but you have to promise not to tell anyone," *you should not commit to that promise.* It is unreasonable for anyone to ask someone to enter into an agreement without knowing the terms of the agreement. Lawyers insist that their clients sign a contract only after they thoroughly understand what will be required of them after signing. When a person writes out a check, he fills in the amount of the check before signing it. In fact, there is a saying that originated from this practice—"Never sign a blank check." If you leave it to the recipient of the check to fill in the amount, you might not have enough money in your account to cover it.

You might consider handling a situation like this in the way a professional counselor would respond. Although counselors are required to maintain confidentiality with their clients, there are two exceptions to this rule of secrecy. A counselor is not required to maintain confidentiality if a client is going to kill herself or someone else. (The second exception, which does not apply to suicide, involves the counselor's knowledge of a child in danger.) We suggest you respond to a friend who asks you to *sign a blank check* by telling her, "I can keep a secret if it doesn't involve someone being killed or hurt." If your friend then refuses to tell you, it is reasonable for you to assume that her secret involves someone's death or injury. In this chapter we are considering suicidal clues. Your friend's refusal would be a clue. You should report this clue to a responsible adult: a teacher, guidance counselor, principal, clergyperson, or parent. If your friend commits suicide you don't want to live with the awareness that you might have been able to prevent it. This is potentially a life-and-death matter.

That he wants to tell you he's thinking about killing himself means he wants help. Nobody is 100 percent suicidal. It might be very small, but there's a part of all suicidal people that wants to be helped and wants to live. As a friend, you should respond to the part of him that's asking for help. Since he needs more help than you are able to provide, help him by getting him the help he needs.

Life is complicated. We try to manage our lives by living according to rules. Keeping our word and not breaking promises is one of those rules. Acting to preserve life is another rule. Sometimes rules come into conflict and we are challenged to choose one over the other. If you've already promised a friend not to tell anyone she's suicidal, we urge you to break that promise. It is better to lose a friendship than a friend. You can repair a broken friendship; you cannot apologize to a friend who is dead.

What if you don't know what to say?

A philosopher once said there's a world of difference between having to say something and having something to say. When a friend announces he's planning his suicide, you will *experience* that difference. You will feel *the need to say something* but realize that you'd better *have something to say*.

You can never go wrong being yourself. You're not a psychiatrist or a trained suicide crisis counselor. You're a friend of someone who is in such pain and confusion that he wants to die. For reasons that we will never fully understand it always helps to talk. Perhaps it is not what is said but the experience of not being alone that eases the pain and diminishes the confusion.

By being with your friend as a friend you are proving to her that she is not alone. By telling her this, perhaps through your tears, you are demonstrating that she is valuable and loved. By promising to continue to spend time with her as a friend, not a counselor, while she's getting the additional help she needs, you are committing to all that you are able to do for her. You can never go wrong being yourself, and a friend is who you are.

What help is available to suicidal people?

There are two ways to respond to this question. One is to tell you *who* is able to help. The other is to tell you *how* suicidal people are helped.

First, ideally a team of helpers is assembled. It's the responsibility of the suicidal person's parents or guardians to contact a mental health professional to develop a plan. If parents deny that a problem exists, then a school guidance counselor or principal will have to meet with them to convince them that professional counseling is needed. Rarely will parents or guardians deny their children a psychological evaluation when contacted by a school counselor or principal.

In addition to parents and other family members providing support at home, friends like you can be involved. It's important that a suicidal person not isolate and recycle his destructive thoughts. Teachers don't have to be told that he is suicidal. They can be told that he's having a difficult time and that they must be patient and understanding about schoolwork. Athletic coaches must also be informed of the need to be especially supportive and less demanding. If your friend has a religious life a clergyperson could provide attention and spiritual guidance. In a team approach each person has a different role to play.

Next we will consider how a suicidal person is helped, and you will see the value of a team approach. There are at least six ways in which a suicidal person can be helped. First, the mobilization of a team consisting of family, friends, teachers, coaches, clergy, and a therapist declares to her that she's not alone. Second, the response by so many people communicates that she is valued. Third, with so much help the problems that had been overwhelming her will seem more manageable. The feeling of being stuck and not knowing what to do will evaporate. Fourth, as she gains a sense of control over her problems, she will acquire more control of her feelings, thoughts, and behavior. Fifth, her counseling will train her in understanding herself and what she can do about certain situations. She will learn the difference between what she can and cannot change. Sixth, she will begin to see herself as you see her: an imperfect but decent and acceptable human being.

Perhaps, even after reading this section, you doubt that there is help for a suicidal person. If so, we ask you to consider that each day a suicidal person moves either toward or away from killing himself. What we have described in this section are changes that will move him away from suicide. Without changes each day there will be movement toward suicide. With a suicidal person, the greatest danger would be to do nothing.

Suicide and homosexuality

Although people from all walks of life kill themselves, suicide occurs more frequently among certain groups. One of these groups is homosexual teenagers.

Chapter 3 presents reasons why some teenagers are suicidal. These reasons apply to both heterosexual and homosexual teenagers. On top of the issues all adolescents have in common, homosexual teens experience additional causes for stress. Unless you are homosexual or wrestling with whether or not you are homosexual you can't know what it is like to be asking questions like:

□ "Am I really a homosexual?"

□ "If I am homosexual, why?"

□ "Should I 'come out' (that is, make my homosexuality known)?"

□ "Some of my friends make jokes about 'gays' and 'queers.' What if they knew about me?"

□ "If I 'come out' what will my family, friends, and teachers think?"

□ "What is life like for a homosexual? What will my future be like? Does my future include AIDS?"

□ "Am I different in a way someone will notice? Will I be discovered?"

□ "Who can I talk to about all of this?"

□ "Why did God make me this way? What does God think about me?"

In the background of all these questions is the awareness with which all of us live. It is the awareness that our acceptance by others depends on conditions we must meet. In spite of talk we've heard about "unconditional love," we realize that such love and acceptance is very rare. It is so rare that sometimes we are tempted to conclude it is nonexistent. "After all," we ask, "don't we have conditions for ourselves for self-acceptance?" The homosexual adolescent wrestles with the question, "Must I be heterosexual to be acceptable to myself and others?"

Homosexual teenagers raised in a family and/or a religious tradition in which it is taught that homosexuality is a sinful choice are finding their struggle even more difficult. Unfortunately in our homophobic culture, fear is generated by ignorance. Only education can halt the fear and unwarranted discrimination against homosexuals. We must ensure that our youth do not become strangers in their own land. For further information, you might contact Gay/Lesbian Youth at (800) 347-TEEN.

Different people have different helping roles to play in the life of a suicidal person. Family members, friends, and the therapist provide support to the one wrestling with suicide. Each can do something to help that the others cannot do. As the friend of a suicidal person, you cannot provide round-the-clock supervision. If that is needed, it's up to the family to provide it. As a friend, you cannot answer complex questions like, "Was I born a homosexual?" A question like that is for a therapist to address.

What you can do as a friend is provide companionship. The gift of your dependable presence in your friend's life prevents aloneness. Miss no opportunity to reassure him that a person is much more than his sexual orientation. Time is a precious thing to give to a person. Any time you give to him reinforces the value of his friendship. A depressed, suicidal person often will try to talk herself into believing that her family is stuck with her and her therapist is paid to be with her. Neither of these things can be said about a friend. As a friend you are there by choice.

Chapter Seven

Religious Questions

One definition of religion is "intensive and comprehensive belief." By this definition a person is religious if he holds a belief deeply ("intensive") that influences every area of his life ("comprehensive"). When tragedy invades a religious person's life, he will have questions for and about God. Even nonreligious people who never attend a church, synagogue, or mosque or read scripture (sacred, religious writings) often have religious questions following a tragedy. A character in the play *The Trial of God* makes this statement following the deaths of his wife and children: "Before tragedy came to my home I never thought of God. Since tragedy's come to my home I can think of nothing but God."

In this chapter the following questions and issues are addressed:

☐ What happens to people when they die?
☐ Why does God allow people to suffer?
☐ Maybe you no longer believe in God.
☐ Who can you talk to about religious questions?

What happens to people when they die?

There are four types of questions: scientific, opinion, debate, and faith. Scientific questions can be answered by laboratory experiments. Opinion questions involve an individual's preferences and tastes. Debate questions are matters that can be argued about without reaching a conclusion. And faith questions require the choice to believe something based on evidence and reason without proof. The question, "What happens to people when they die?" is a faith question.

Theoretically there are five possible answers to this question. One, perhaps the most appealing, is agnosticism. This is the belief that the answer to this question cannot be known until we die. A second is annihilation, the belief that we have no conscious existence in death. Our bodies decompose but we are not aware of it. A third possibility is universalism, the belief that there is a heaven and all people go there to be with God for eternity. Some religions teach a fourth belief. This is the teaching that following God's judgment some people spend eternity in heaven and others are condemned to eternal separation from God. (This eternal separation is commonly referred to as hell.) The fifth theoretical possibility is reincarnation, the belief that we return to live another life in another body.

After reading the previous paragraph it's easy to understand why the afterlife question is a matter of faith. (It can also be a matter for debate.) Which of the five beliefs a person holds will be the result of several factors. Family discussions, education, and religious teaching may have influenced your thinking about this question. Also, what you've experienced, especially the death of someone you love, may have influenced your thoughts and feelings on this matter.

However you direct your faith in answering the afterlife question, keep in mind that faith is a living thing. Like all living things it grows and changes. As you learn and experience more, your faith will be refined. Faith not only helps you to understand your experiences; it is also affected by what you experience. In this chapter we suggest whom you can talk to about faith questions.

Why does God allow people to suffer?

This, too, is a faith question. It is one of the most challenging questions for people who believe in God as One who is good, loving, and powerful. In wrestling with this question some people have concluded that God is good and loving but not powerful enough to prevent suffering. Others have said God is good, loving, and powerful but is not involved in the lives of people. This belief, called deism, describes God as the Creator and Observer of human beings.

Others have concluded that God will not interfere with the free will or power of choice of human beings. However, this explanation doesn't address the suffering caused by disease and natural disasters. Some people have decided that human suffering proves that God's existence is irrelevant to our lives. "If God does exist," they ask, "what difference does it make?" And some people have concluded that the reality and intensity of suffering in the world proves that God doesn't exist. What you conclude about God and suffering will be an expression of your faith.

Probably you've realized that none of these opinions provides a complete answer to the question of God and suffering. As you work on your own answer it will be helpful to consider the answers others have offered.

Maybe you no longer believe in God

Sometimes the emotional damage caused by an experience is sufficient to drive a person to the conclusion that there is no God. One person cannot tell another what to feel. When one is suffering, the words "You mustn't feel that way" provide no pain relief.

As you read these words maybe you are in such pain that you no longer believe in God. We are not going to tell you that you must believe in God. That wouldn't be any more helpful than telling you to stop feeling your pain. Instead of speaking to you about feelings we have a few simple suggestions that might help you in dealing with your pain.

First, this may not be the time to sort out whether or not God exists. Even for people who believe in God there are times when their feelings seem to scream: "There is no God." It's also true that even people who deny God's existence sometimes experience feelings that tell them, "There is a God."

Second, our beliefs come from our thoughts, feelings, and experiences. As we live, we have experiences. We use what we know and feel to make sense of our experiences. In fact, much of our lives is spent making sense of the things that happen to us and others. You do not have a lifetime commitment to anything you believe today. As your feelings change and knowledge increases, you may change your mind. There is a word to describe this process: *growth*.

Third, it would be good for you to talk to people who care about you even if their beliefs about God differ from yours. Anyone who is concerned about you and wants to help you will not engage you in a theological debate. (The person who is determined to debate with you isn't really interested in helping you.) In the next section we suggest several people you can talk to about religious questions. However, if you don't want to talk about religious questions, don't cut yourself off from a religious person you know who loves you.

Who you can talk to about religious questions

In this chapter we've raised religious questions: What happens to people when they die? Why does God allow people to suffer? What if you no longer believe in God? Now we raise a fourth question that's related to the other three: To whom do you go to discuss religious questions?

Choosing a person with whom to discuss religious questions involves several considerations. You might ask yourself, "Are this person's beliefs in line with mine?" And, more importantly, "Can I relate to her? Will I feel comfortable sharing my questions and innermost feelings?"

Of course clergypeople are knowledgeable about religion. But clergypeople, especially from different faiths, and even within the same faith, often disagree. Nevertheless, since you have to begin with someone, begin by considering the priest, minister, or rabbi you already know. If you don't know a clergyperson consider contacting the one who performed the funeral service for your friend. Another possibility would be to ask someone you respect to recommend a person with whom you could discuss religious questions. Or one of your friends might be able to suggest someone with whom he's had a good experience. If none of these suggestions are workable for you, there remain at least two more possibilities: radio and newspaper. It might take some time, but you can become familiar with clergypeople by listening to religious broadcasts and reading the religion section of your local newspaper. These are ways of becoming familiar with someone who seems compassionate and intelligent who might be able to help you.

An important part of personality is a person's style of relating. The second thing to consider when looking for a person to talk to is whether or not she's a good listener. Good listeners listen more than they speak. Good listeners ask questions to make sure they've heard what you've said. They will ask you to repeat or rephrase what you've said to make sure they've understood you correctly. Good listeners answer clearly the question asked and ask if you're satisfied with the answer they've given.

A very important characteristic of a helpful person is his willingness to say, "I don't know." Don't be surprised if an intelligent, educated person admits to not knowing something. The person who really wants to help is likely to say, "Although I don't know the answer to your question, I'm going to try to find it and get back to you."

Don't be reluctant to ask a person to speak with you. For clergy and nonclergy alike, it is an honor to be asked to help someone.

Chapter Eight

Popular Misconceptions about Suicide

At this moment you are doing something most people will never do: you are reading a book about suicide. Many people think they know about suicide without ever having read anything about it. Perhaps they believe this because of the many ideas about suicide that have circulated for so long they've become accepted as facts. In this chapter we discuss several popular misconceptions about suicide. In trying to make sense of your friend's suicide it is important that you work with facts rather than myths. In this chapter, we will confront the following misconceptions:

- □ People who talk about suicide don't commit suicide.
- □ People who attempt suicide are just looking for attention.
- □ Suicide runs in families.
- □ People who commit suicide leave behind a note.
- □ People commit suicide because they are depressed.

This chapter also includes two factors that may have been a part of your friend's suicide:

- □ Your friend had everything going for him.
- □ Your friend had been sad but seemed to be getting better.

People who talk about suicide don't commit suicide

People who talk about suicide may also attempt and accomplish suicide. In fact, talking about suicide is one of the clues provided by a suicidal person. This doesn't mean that everyone who talks about suicide will eventually attempt it. (In the next section of this chapter we consider people who talk about killing themselves to get attention.) Also, there are people who commit suicide without ever having talked about it.

Human behavior is very complicated. It is too complex to allow us to make a statement that will apply to all people. The statement that people who talk about suicide don't commit suicide has too many exceptions for it to be a rule.

People who attempt suicide are just looking for attention

There will always be people who talk about and even attempt suicide at least partly in order to get attention. But since many people who commit suicide have a record of previous attempts, it would be unwise to believe that all people who commit suicide do so in their first attempt.

Some people are not very good at planning things, including their suicide. Many suicide attempts fail because of an overdose of pills that are not lethal or a car that withstood a crash. One of the reasons why medical doctors have a surprisingly high rate of suicide themselves is that they don't make mistakes when overdosing. Also, there are many cases of people surviving suicide attempts that seemed almost certain to kill them. The ability of the human body to survive trauma is almost incredible.

When dealing with a person who has attempted suicide, it's not the most important thing to determine whether or not he did it for attention. Either you have a person who actually wants to die or one who desperately wants to be heard. Whichever is the case, you're dealing with someone who needs to be heard. You're dealing with someone who needs professional help.

Suicide runs in families

Again, there is no suicide gene. Suicide is not inherited in the way that eye color or intelligence is. However, depression, which contributes to suicide, can be inherited. Not all depression is inherited. A lot of people are depressed because of their life circumstances.

If depression runs in a person's family and one of the family members commits suicide, then an example has been set. This example can influence other family members, especially children, if the suicide was that of a parent. We know of one doctor who asked a suicidal mother, "Will you go home and write a letter telling your daughter whenever she feels sad she should consider killing herself?" When the woman refused, saying that such a letter would be outrageous, the doctor told her that her suicide would be the same as that letter. Once suicide is introduced into the family as a problem-solving technique, it is more likely to be considered an option by other family members.

People who commit suicide
leave behind a note

When there's news of a suicide it's not unusual to hear people ask, "What did she say in her suicide note?" There's a common belief that before killing herself a person shares her reason for her suicide. The fact is that only one in four suicides includes a note.

We said in Chapter 2 that some suicides are impulsive, meaning that they occurred suddenly with little or no planning. Another reason for so few suicide notes is that by the time a person kills himself he is exhausted from the struggle to live and has only enough energy left for the final act.

People commit suicide
because they are depressed

It's unlikely that anyone would disagree with this statement. It's included in this chapter on misconceptions because although it's true, it's an incomplete and misleading statement.

Of course people who commit suicide are depressed. However, not all depressed people commit suicide. Until we understand the difference between a depressed person who kills herself and one who doesn't, to say "People who commit suicide are depressed" is to say next to nothing. A truly helpful study of the relationship between depression and suicide would answer the following questions:

☐ Is there a difference in the causes of depression between depressed people who commit suicide and those who don't?

☐ Is there a difference in the treatments of depression received by those who commit suicide compared to those who don't?

☐ Do depressed people who commit suicide understand and talk about their depression differently from those who don't?

☐ Depression is one thing and suicide is another. Is there a *third thing* that leads to both depression *and* suicide for some people but only depression in others?

To say that people who commit suicide are depressed and leave it at that is misleading. That explanation can lead people to believe that eventually all depressed people commit suicide. The fact is most depressed people do not kill themselves. More than 80 percent of people diagnosed with depression seek treatment, are helped, and do not commit suicide.

Anorexia nervosa is an eating disorder in which a person refuses to eat. Believing that "People who commit suicide are depressed" is like believing that "People who die from anorexia nervosa don't eat enough." Of course those who die from anorexia nervosa starve to death. But most people with anorexia nervosa don't starve to death. The crucial question is, "What is the difference between those who die and those who recover?" If you heard that someone drowned you wouldn't accept "He was swimming" as an adequate explanation. You'd want to know, "What else happened?" For a suicide, "He was depressed" is an insufficient answer.

Your friend had everything going for him (or her)

In Chapter 6 we included the description of Dallas Cowboys football star Deion Sanders's attempted suicide. If there's anyone who has everything going for him it is Deion Sanders. An all-pro defensive back on one of America's most popular teams, Sanders is an exceptional athlete. Actually, he's more than exceptional, he's remarkable. For several years he managed two sports careers, also playing major league baseball as an outfielder with the New York Yankees, Atlanta Braves, and Cincinnati Reds. Needless to say, Sanders is a multimillionaire. He is also the survivor of an attempted suicide.

No matter how gifted and successful a person is, he experiences pain and disappointment like everyone else. In Deion Sanders's case he was despondent over his father's recent death. It is not unusual for a person who has everything going for him to expect a great deal from himself. A popular saying from the Christian Bible is "To whom much is given, much is required." The person who sets high goals for himself is just as likely to experience failure as anybody else.

Finally, a well-known quotation from a famous philosopher is "Most men lead lives of quiet desperation." When a philosopher's quotation has become well known it's because it's captured a truth about life. We are always on the outside of another person's life. As observers we can never know what's going on in the mind and heart of another human being. The thoughts and feelings of another are available to us only if that person chooses to share them. In the movie *Good Will Hunting*, a young man's psychologist appeals to him with the words, "I can't know you if you don't talk to me." Did you ever feel like saying those words to your friend? If you did you may have sensed her quiet desperation.

Your friend had been sad but seemed to be getting better

Perhaps the most deceptive feature of your friend's suicide was the appearance that he was getting better. It is not unusual for someone who has struggled long with the question "To be or not to be?" to experience great relief when the decision to die has been made. This relief gives others the impression that he is getting better.

If shortly before killing herself your friend seemed to have "snapped out of it," it's likely she was experiencing the relief that came with the realization that the long, agonizing battle to live was over.

Chapter Nine

And Now, the Future

A popular saying these days is "Get a life!" Actually, you don't have to get a life because you *already have one.* In this chapter we want to help you consider your future while remembering the past. Since your friend will always be a part of your life it is important that his place in the years ahead bring honor to him and warmth to you. In this chapter we consider the following:

☐ Letting go and getting on with your life.
☐ Rebuilding your life.
☐ Treasuring your memories.
☐ Growing through grief.
☐ Recognizing when you need help and how to find it.

One definition of life is, "Life is what happens to you after you've planned something else." Your friend's suicide is something you didn't plan on and it's brought pain and confusion into your life. In this chapter we consider how life with pain and confusion can be managed.

Letting go and getting on with your life

There are many things people say to one another intending to help that really don't make sense. Perhaps you've been told to "Try harder to put this behind you." What does it mean to *try harder*? We can try harder to lift something or to run faster, but those are physical activities. If "to put this behind you" means to make up your mind to forget it, this is impossible. That would be like trying to lose weight by continuously saying to yourself, "I'm not going to think about food." Enough said about things that don't help. Let's move on to things that do help.

It is important that you recognize your feelings. It will be helpful to you to be honest about what you are feeling. Making believe you aren't sad or missing your friend is not helpful. The sooner you identify what you are feeling the sooner you will understand why you have that feeling. You will then be able to do something positive about what you are feeling. For example, if several months from now you wake up feeling extremely depressed you might ask yourself, "Why am I so sad today?" The answer might be that today is your friend's birthday. Knowing why you're feeling such sadness you decide to make that day one of the two or three days a year you go to the cemetery. Or you write a note to your friend's parents or brother letting them know you are remembering her this day.

The formula for managing feelings in a positive way is to *identify, know,* and *act*. Earlier in this book we said that it isn't necessary to know why something helps in order for it to be helpful. Perhaps this formula works because it is located between the extremes of denial and indulgence. Denial would be to make believe a feeling doesn't exist. Indulgence would be to carry on as though it's the only feeling that exists. Often the best place to find yourself is between two extreme positions. Whatever the reason, it is enough to know that the *identify, know,* and *act* strategy is helpful.

Again we encounter a phrase that isn't helpful. What does it mean to "get over" something? If you were a high jumper at a track meet, "getting over it" would mean clearing the high jump bar. But what does it mean to "get over" emotional pain and psychological confusion?

Unlike the high jumper who clears the bar once and for all, you are involved in a continual process. In chapter 5 we referred to this process as mourning. Mourning takes time. One of the most helpful things you can do for yourself is to focus on the next thing you need to do and do it. Mourning is not a time for looking at long-range plans or making lists of things to do. In the popular movie *Sleepless in Seattle*, a young father who recently lost his wife to cancer is asked, "So what are you going to do now?" His answer describes what it means to focus on the next thing: "What am I going to do? I'm going to get up tomorrow morning and breathe until I don't have to think about breathing anymore. And I'll try not to think about how I had it 'almost perfect' for a while."

During mourning, life is best planned in twenty-four-hour segments. As mourning continues, eventually you will notice that the intensity of your pain and the depth of your confusion have diminished.

Rebuilding your life

It might be helpful and even encouraging for you to think about the word *rebuilding* in a different setting. Rebuilding is what communities do after a hurricane. Rebuilding is what a city does following a war. How do communities and cities rebuild?

First, they separate what must be done immediately from things that can wait. Second, they get to work on those immediate needs. And third, they gradually take care of those things that have waited as time and energy allows.

Using this approach, what would these three phases look like in your life? If you find it difficult to answer this question you might want to get help. Talk to someone about the things you need to do, separating them from those that can wait.

Also, as you rebuild, don't act too quickly. Don't quit an athletic team or other extracurricular activity. If you need some time away, try to arrange for a leave of absence for a week or two. Don't drop any courses because of the workload or because it's a class that reminds you of your friend. Instead, try to negotiate extra time for assignments either directly with the teacher or indirectly through the guidance counselor.

We strongly suggest that you involve your parents in the rebuilding process. You are adjusting to a life that no longer includes your friend. The time, energy, and caring that you put into that relationship is in the process of being redirected. This process is so gradual that you might not even notice that it's happening. But it is happening and the support of your parents is important at this time.

Treasuring your memories

Your friend killed himself, cutting short a life that included pain. In your sadness has it occurred to you that your friendship may have enabled him to live longer with less pain? His suicide is a tragedy and it always will be. But there is more to his life than the pain he lived with and the way he died. Your friendship brought him pleasure amidst pain and probably encouraged him to live longer than he would have had he not known you.

While she struggled to live, your presence in her life prevented your friend from being alone. That was a great gift to her, and she appreciated it. As friends, you cried and laughed together—that's what friends do. Even though her suicide ended her life, there were times when life seemed worth living to her. You were a part of those better times.

You will never forget how your friend died. You'll not have to work to remember that. But in your mourning and the years ahead, remember the things you did together, times you laughed together, and those serious and hilarious conversations. Treasure your memories.

Growing through grief

Anything we could say to you that would fit on a bumper sticker probably isn't worth reading. Philosophers and writers through the centuries have produced countless quotations about the benefits of suffering. You've seen or will be seeing many of them framed and hanging on walls, written in greeting cards, decorating coffee mugs, and posted in locker rooms and classrooms to inspire and motivate. Since you'll be seeing too many of them in the years ahead, we're not going to provide any here.

Instead we offer this thought concerning the pain known as grief. If you were indifferent to your friend, then you would feel nothing from his death. The gain you felt by welcoming a person into your life brought with it the risk of losing that person. There is pain when someone or something of value is lost. Now you are familiar with that pain. To become familiar with something new is to grow. You did not ask for this growth. You did nothing to cause this growth. We can offer no profound thought about this relationship between pain and growth. We simply say that this is an unavoidable condition of life on this planet.

Recognizing when you need help and how to find it

If two full months have gone by since your friend's suicide and any of the following statements describes you then you need help:

- ☐ I'm no more functional in meeting my responsibilities now than two months ago.
- ☐ I'm isolating from my family and friends.
- ☐ Nothing seems to hold my interest, I tend to drift away from whatever I'm doing.
- ☐ I'm not eating well. (Or, I'm eating too much.)
- ☐ I'm not sleeping well. (Or, I'm sleeping too much.)
- ☐ I'm not interested in things that used to be fun.
- ☐ I have no sense of humor and being with me is not much fun.

□ I've been drinking and/or using drugs lately. It's about the only relief I've found.

□ I've been accident-prone lately.

□ I've been biting my nails (or pulling out my hair or digging at my skin) lately.

□ I've started (or returned to or increased) cigarette smoking.

□ I've been thinking about suicide, wondering if I'm feeling the way my friend felt before she did it.

You can get help by asking for it. Since we don't know who is available to you we are going to suggest categories of people. We are recommending them in the order in which you might seek them. If you don't think you could approach the person we've suggested, then consider the next one listed.

1. Parents
2. Other *adult* relative
3. Family doctor
4. Clergyperson
5. School guidance counselor
6. Teacher or athletic coach
7. *Older* brother or sister

Chapter Ten

Conclusion:
Suggested Materials and Resources

After you have read these pages, it is our hope that you may better understand some of your confused emotions as well as some of the reasons why a friend has deliberately taken his life.

Despite your friendship, you are different from the one who died. Suicide does not have to be your way out of difficult situations. While you may regret some things that you have said or done, it is important to remember that you probably did the best you could.

You cannot control someone else's life. You are not responsible for someone else's destiny—only your own. You are not to blame. It's not your fault.

If you give yourself time, your pain will diminish. You will begin to heal. You are in the process of healing, even if it doesn't feel like healing. Neither the best nor the worst of feelings is permanent. If you are hurting as you are reading these words, embrace the truth that your pain will lessen in time.

If suicide is described as the desire to die, then this book may provide you with the will to live and tools to cope through difficult times.

We firmly believe that each life is unique, special, and worth preserving. When you feel alone, frustrated, stressed; when problems at home or school seem so overwhelming; when a friend confides that he is thinking of suicide; when you, yourself, think that you would be better off dead—

Break the Silence!

Break the silence and the emotional momentum by availing yourself of the following resources:

- □ Hot-lines
- □ Suicide prevention resources

- [ ] Mental health and depression resources
- [ ] Crisis intervention and support directories
- [ ] Helpful reading materials
- [ ] Books to share with your teachers
- [ ] Audio-visual support

Hot-lines

In the United States, call 1-800-252-TEEN. Your call will be toll-free and completely confidential. The counseling staff consists of trained, understanding teenagers and adults who will listen without judging or giving unwanted advice. Calls are received 24 hours a day.

In Canada, call 1–800–668–6868 for Kids Help Phone, Canada's only toll-free national telephone counseling service for children and youth. The site offers a forum for kids experiencing violence (either at home or in their communities), struggling with alcohol and/or drug abuse, and dealing with issues related to suicide.

Suicide prevention resources

American Suicide Foundation
(212) 363–3500
Voice: (202) 237–2280
Fax: (202) 237–2282
Internet: http://www.suicidology.org/
E-Mail: amyjomc@ix.netcom.com

AAS promotes research, public awareness programs, education, and training for professionals and volunteers. This site includes things you should know about suicide, membership information, a listing of AAS publications, and conference information.

American Foundation for Suicide Prevention (AFSP)
120 Wall Street, 22nd Floor
New York, NY 10005
Phone: (212) 363-3500
Fax: (212) 363-6237
Toll-Free: (888) 333-AFSP
Internet: http://www.afsp.org/
The AFSP is dedicated to advancing our knowledge of suicide and our ability to prevent it. This is a comprehensive site covering many aspects of suicide and related topics for those seeking information for educational or research purposes. Information is provided on topics from assisted suicide, suicide, and AIDS to depression and available support.

Canadian Association for Suicide Prevention
c/o The Support Network
#301, 11456 Jasper Avenue NW
Edmonton, Alberta T5K OM1
Canada
Phone: (413) 782-0198
Fax: (403) 488-1495
Internet: http://www.compusmart.ab.ca/supnet/casp.htm
E-Mail: casp@compusmart.ab.ca
CASP/ACPS is a nonprofit national association consisting of individuals from all walks of life. CASP/ACPS's mandate is to advocate for and encourage the development of suicide prevention, in-

tervention, and postvention activities on a national level, and to unite people across Canada's diverse set of cultures in an effort to understand suicide and reduce its impact.

Light for Life Foundation of America
P.O. Box 644
Westminster, CO 80030-0644
Phone: (303) 429-3530
Fax: (303) 426-4496
Internet: http://yellowribbon.org/
E-Mail: light4life@yellowribbon.org
This suicide prevention site provides information on the Yellow Ribbon Program for preventing youth suicide. Also included are suicide facts and statistics.

The Samaritans
10 The Grove
Slough, Berkshire SL1 1QP
United Kingdom
Phone: 01753 532713
Fax: 01753 775787
Internet: http://www.cmhc.com/samaritans/
E-Mail: samaritans@anon.twwells.com

Suicide Awareness/Voices of Education (SA/VE)
P.O. Box 24507
Minneapolis, MS 55424-0507
Phone: (612) 946-7998
Internet: http://www.save.org/index.html/
E-Mail: save@winternet.com
The mission of SA/VE is to educate about suicide and to speak for suicide survivors.

Suicide Information & Education Centre
#201, 1615 10th Ave. SW
Calgary, Alberta T3C 0J7
Canada
Internet: http//www.siec.ca/
E-Mail: info@siec.ca

Suicide Prevention Advocacy Network (SPAN)
5034 Odin's Way
Marietta, GA 30068
Phone: (888) 649-1419
Fax: (770) 642-1419
Internet: http://www.spanusa.org/
SPAN is a United States-based network of persons working to raise national awareness and advocate for the development of a proven, effective suicide prevention program. This site features their newsletter, community organizing tips, excerpts from advocacy letters, and legal information.

Mental health and depression resources

Canadian Mental Health Association (CMHA), Alberta Division
328 Capital Place
9707 110 Street
Edmonton, Alberta T5K 2L9
Canada
Phone: (403) 482-6576
Fax: (403) 482-6348
E-Mail: division@alberta.cmha.ca
The CMHA is a national voluntary network of 135 branches in communities across Canada. They are dedicated to the promotion

of the mental health of all people. Information on Alberta's mental health system, a discussion forum, and resources on mental health and mental illness can be found at this site.

Canadian Mental Health Association (CMHA), Toronto Branch
Metro Office: 970 Lawrence Avenue West, Suite 205
Toronto, Ontario M6A 3B6
Canada
Phone: (416) 789-7957
Fax: (416) 789-9079
East Metro Office: 1200 Markham Road, Suite 500
Scarborough, Ontario M1H 3C3
Canada
Phone: (416) 289-6285
Fax: (416) 289-6843
Internet: http://www3.sympatico.ca/cmha.toronto/home.htm
E-Mail: cmha.toronto@sympatico.ca
This web site contains: links to CMHA branches across Canada, and descriptions of useful pamphlets and books dealing with a wide variety of life's emotional challenges. Topics include grief, stress, parenting, divorce, suicide, depression, and many others.

Depression Resources List
http://www.execpc.com/-corbeau/
This site includes links to Internet support groups, mailing lists, and forums for those who suffer from depression. Information on suicide covers prevention, warning signs, self-injury, and where to get help. It is compiled and maintained by Dennis Taylor.

National Mental Health Association (NMHA)
1021 Prince Street
Alexandria, VA 22314
TTY: 1-800-433-5959

Phone: 1-800-969-NHMA (6642)
Fax: (888) 836-6070
Internet: http://www.nmha.org/infoctr/indx.cfm
E-Mail: infoctr@nmha.org
The NMHA is dedicated to improving the mental health of all in-
dividuals and achieving victory over mental illness. This web site
contains two useful fact sheets covering suicide warning signs, risk
factors, crisis intervention, and helping suicidal teens.

Crisis intervention and support directories

☐ Suicide Prevention/Crisis Intervention Directory for
listing of 600 current crisis agencies in the
United States and Canada.
☐ Directory of Survivor Support Groups for listing of cur-
rent survivor support groups in the United States
and Canada.
Contact: American Association of Suicidology, 4201 Connecticut
Avenue, NW, Suite 310, Washington, DC 20008

Helpful reading materials

Alexander, Victori. *Words I Never Thought to Speak*. New
York: Lexington Press, 1991.
Individual journeys through grief after suicide affording survivors
both voice and meaning for their tragic losses.
Bolton, Iris. *My Son . . . My Son; A Guide to Healing After
Death, Loss, or Suicide*. Atlanta: Bolton Press, 1983.

A therapist describes her emotions following her son's suicide, with pathways to healing.

Chance, Sue, M.D. *Stronger than Death: When Suicide Touches Your Life*. New York: Avon Books, 1992.

Coleman, Loren. *Suicide Clusters*. Boston and London: Faber and Faber, 1987.

Derrek, Kirsten. *Dancing With the Skeletons*. Omaha, NE: Centering Corporation, 1995.
Affirming and comforting meditations for suicide survivors.

Gordon, Sol. *When Living Hurts*. New York: Union of Genevian Hebrew Congregations, 1985.
A lively what-to-do book for teenagers who feel discouraged, sad, hopeless, frustrated, depressed, suicidal.

Grollman, Earl A. *Bereaved Children and Teens*. Boston: Beacon Press, 1995.
"In this much needed book a discussion of the complex problems faced by young people when death explodes." —Sherwin B. Nuland, M.D., National Book Award Winner.

Grollman, Earl A. *Straight Talk about Death for Teenagers*. Boston: Beacon Press, 1993.
"I wish I could send this book to every one of the thousands of teens who write me in their pain and confusion over death." — Beth Winship, "Ask Beth" syndicated columnist.

Grollman, Earl A. *Suicide: Prevention, Intervention, Postvention*. Boston: Beacon Press, 1988.
Recognizing the warning signs of suicide, how to intervene, and when necessary, consoling family and friends who have lost a loved one to suicide.

Grollman, Earl A. *Talking about Death: A Dialogue between Parent and Child*. Boston: Beacon Press, 1990.
"An important resource for grieving children." —Fred Rogers, "Mr. Rogers' Neighborhood."

Kent, Jack. *There's No Such Thing as a Dragon*. New York: Golden Press, 1975.
Unfortunately this book is out of print. Fortunately it is available. Ask at a bookstore or a library how to acquire out-of-print books. It will be worth the effort to get this children's story (for all ages) about the importance and value of talking about problems. We strongly recommend this book.

Klagsbrun, Francine. *Youth and Suicide: Too Young to Die*. New York: Pocket Books, 1977.
Sensitive practical advice in recognizing and dealing with adolescents' cries for help.

Ross, E. Betsy. *After Suicide: A Ray of Hope*. Iowa City: Lynn Publications, 1990.
Helping oneself and family after the event of suicide.

Sexton-Jones, Sondra. *This is Survivable: When Someone You Love Commits Suicide*. Omaha, NE: Centering Corporation, 1996.
How love and compassionate support can bring healing after a beloved takes his or her life.

Styron, William. *Darkness Visible: A Memoir of Madness*. New York: Vintage Books, Random House, 1990.

Traisman, Enid S. *Fire in My Heart, Ice In My Veins*. Omaha, NE: Centering Corporation, 1992.
A creative journal for teenagers to work through the grieving process.

Westberg, Granger. *Good Grief: A Constructive Approach to the Problem of Loss*. Philadelphia: Fortress Press, 1962.
A champion boxer once said, "It's the punch you don't see coming that knocks you down." This book briefly and clearly describes "the punches" by walking you through ten stages of mourning.

Wolterstorff, Nicholas. *Lament for a Son*. Grand Rapids, MI: W. B. Eerdman's Publishing House, 1995.
The language of grief does not come easily. The author expresses

his pain at the loss of his son in a mountain-climbing accident. People who have read this book have told us this man has found the words we couldn't find to express our thoughts and feelings.

Books to share with your teachers

Johnston, Jerry. *Why Suicide? What Parents and Teachers Must Know to Save Our Kids*. Overland Park, KS: Johnston Association, 1987.
A school's understanding of suicide through increased awareness and better education.

Stevenson, Robert. *What Will We Do? Preparing a School Community to Cope with Crises*. New York: Baywood, 1994.
Perhaps the best book to help students, staff, parents, and community with the crisis of death.

Underwood, Maureen M., and Karen Dunn-Maxim. *Managing Sudden Traumatic Loss in the Schools*. Revised Edition. Piscataway, NJ: UMD of New Jersey, 1997.
A must-read manual compiled by the New Jersey Suicide Prevention Project.

Zalaznik, Patricia H. *Dimensions of Loss and Death Education Curriculum and Resource Guide*. Minneapolis: Abundant Resources, 1997.
An outstanding and well-organized resource guide, workbook, and curriculum for death education in the school system.

Audio-visual support

In these straightforward videos, through the dimension of sight and sound, you will witness the stories of the pain and healing of those challenged by suicide.

Choices—A Suicide Prevention Program.
This video tells the story of an at-risk teenager, interwoven with real-life experiences of other adolescents who have attempted to take their own lives. 1996, 18 minutes. Aquarius Health Care Videos, Sherborn, Massachusetts 01770.

Dead Poets Society.
A high school senior concludes suicide is the only way to free himself from a dilemma. Robin Williams brilliantly portrays the boy's inspiring English teacher.

Family Ties, "Greg's Death."
This video isn't available in video stores so you'll have to be on the lookout for the episode from the television series reruns. Alex Keaton, played by Michael J. Fox, will have you moving back and forth between tears and laughter as he processes the accidental death of his best friend.

Depression: A Treatable Disease.
From their stories, we hear the stress that depression places on families, and learn meaningful methods to cope. 1991, 26 minutes. Aquarius Health Care Videos, Sherborn, Massachusetts 01770.

Good Will Hunting.
A young genius with a history that includes severe physical abuse is challenged by his psychologist and his girlfriend to talk about himself and let them into his life.

It's a Wonderful Life.
You may already have seen this movie classic. The benefit to you will be its exploration of the meaning of life and how it can be missed by not seeing the obvious and ordinary.

Living with Loss; Healing with Hope.
Compiled from the works of Earl A. Grollman, the comforting visuals and music of nature with supporting words of healing. 1995, 12 minutes. National Music Service, Inc., Spokane, Washington 99207.

Lost and Found: Young People Talk about Depression.
A powerful and diverse video featuring eight young people from ages 11 to 20 who discuss the sources, impact, and aftermath of their depression. 1996, 21 minutes. Aquarius Health Care Videos, Sherborn, Massachusetts 01770.

No Easy Way: Coping with a Loved One's Suicide.
Even in the face of the trauma of suicide, you will see how each survivor copes with the tragic loss. 1995, 30 minutes. Aquarius Health Care Videos, Sherborn, Massachusetts 01770.

Ordinary People.
This movie, which won an Academy Award for Best Picture, first appeared as a book written by Judith Guest. In it a high school senior struggles with guilt, depression, and suicidality following his surviving the boating accident in which his brother drowned.

Teen Grief: Climbing Back.
A powerful and intimate look at the experience of thirteen young people as they explore their grief process. 1993, 23 minutes. Hospice of Metro Denver, Denver, Colorado 80209.

Teen Grief: A Guide for Adults.
The teen grief process with essential insights for facilitating an adolescent support group. 1994, 22 minutes. Hospice of Metro Denver, Denver, Colorado 80209.

The Stigma of Mental Illness.
Available through the Carter Foundation in Atlanta, Georgia, this video can be borrowed for no rental fee at Blockbuster Video's Community Service section. The highlight of this 20-minute presentation is Academy Award-winning actor Rod Steiger's dramatic reading of an essay he wrote when he was contemplating suicide.

For the most comprehensive materials dealing with programs, agencies, and organizations, we recommend Richard Gilbert's *Responding to Grief: A Complete Resource Guide* (Point Richmond, CA: The Spirit of Health, 1997).

3/01 1 4/00
5/03 4 4/03